POETRY

AND

THE RENASCENCE OF WONDER

POETRY

AND THE

RENASCENCE OF WONDER

BY
THEODORE
WATTS-DUNTON

KENNIKAT PRESS
Port Washington, N. Y./London

POETRY AND THE RENASCENCE OF WONDER

First published in 1916
Reissued in 1970 by Kennikat Press
Library of Congress Catalog Card No: 78-105847
ISBN 0-8046-1057-6

Manufactured by Taylor Publishing Company   Dallas, Texas

INTRODUCTION

I T was my special privilege to be on intimate terms of friendship with the author for more than forty years. Soon after our first meeting at the house of my father, Dr. Gordon Hake, the " parable poet," we became in 1873, joint occupiers of a set of chambers in Great James Street, near Holborn. Here we had Swinburne for a neighbour, who, being at that moment engaged in the writing of *Bothwell*, invited us on many an occasion to assist at his readings from the " *drame èpique.*" It was in this " bardic atmosphere " in London that Watts-Dunton began to write on poetic criticism for the literary journals. His first essay, *The Lost Hamlet*, appeared at this time in the *New Monthly Magazine*. After a year's residence in Great James Street, we took a set of rooms in Danes' Inn ; and it was now that my friend joined the *Examiner*, then under the editorship of Professor Minto. It was through Watts-Dunton's literary relations with Minto as will be seen, that he came to be invited

to write the essay on " Poetry " for the *Encyclopædia Britannica ;* and it was through his
success as a contributor to Minto's journal
that Norman MacColl, then editor of the
Athenæum, " discovered " Theodore Watts, as
he was then called, and induced him to become
a member of his staff.

Watts-Dunton soon came to be regarded
by everyone in the literary circles in which he
moved as an authority on the subject of poetic
art. He won this distinctive mark not merely
through his criticisms on the poets of the period
in the *Examiner* and afterwards in the *Athenæum.* The " Wednesday evening " gatherings
at Danes' Inn did still more to convince those
who heard his " talks on poetry " that he was
thoroughly conversant with the laws of versification, and possessed, moreover, an exceptional
knowledge of the history of poetry. Persian
tales, with their fascinating poetic motives,
appealed to him in a marked degree, inspiring
the subject for more than one sonnet in his
volume " The Coming of Love."

The truth is, as he told me in our thousand
and one quiet talks together in Danes' Inn,
that in his earliest days he conceived the bold
idea of writing a comprehensive treatise on the

history of poetry ; and when barely nineteen years of age, soon after leaving school, he began to devote many an hour during his solitary walks by the river Ouse, in the neighbourhood of his native town of St. Ives, to meditations over this project. The ambitious design, as far as he achieved it, may be said to represent the chief occupation of a lifetime.

When he left St. Ives and came to reside with me in London, he was already a middle-aged man. With him he brought his treatise on Poetry in rough manuscript form. It by no means covered the broad field contemplated in the first flush of youthful enthusiasm; even the portions dealing with the first principles of poetic art seemed to him, an exceptionally conscientious worker, to need further revision. But finding himself busily engaged in journalism, while at the same time continuing to follow his profession as a solicitor, those spare moments which he had thought to bestow upon the treatise proved lamentably insufficient.

It so chanced, however, that while still upon the staff of the *Examiner*, he learnt from Professor Minto that Thomas S. Baynes had been selected by Messrs. A. and C. Black, the Edinburgh publishers, to edit the ninth edition of the *Encyclopædia Britannica,* and that this recently-appointed editor was in search of a writer competent to undertake the article on Poetry ; for the new edition of the work was to be almost entirely re-arranged and re-written, fundamentally different, in fact, from the previous editions, and all other previous editions. Professor Baynes was not long in deciding that " Theodore Watts " was the best informed man for the purpose. The editor certainly had had serious thoughts of inviting either Swinburne or Matthew Arnold to write the essay, but he came to realise in time that both these poets had given their attention principally to the historic method of criticism, and that method did not appeal to the editor as likely to meet the requirements of a publication of this description. What he sought to secure was an article setting forth as briefly as possible the nature, functions, and forms of poetry ; an article in a word, that would not occupy more than eight or ten pages of the *Encyclopædia Britannica.* After some hesitation, Watts-Dunton undertook to supply the article. The material—far more material than was needed —was ready at hand. His hesitation simply arose from this fact ; he began to realise how

hampered he would be as to space ; owing to
these " space restrictions " he would be forced
not only to delete at least two-thirds of his
treatise as comprised in the original manuscript form, but would also have to leave the
conclusion of the argument undeveloped. In
this unavoidably compressed shape, Watts-
Dunton's essay on " Poetry " was written, in
1884, and appeared in the ninth edition of the
Encyclopædia. It was reproduced in the two
subsequent editions without any important
alterations. The article has been described by
the author himself as " a brief essay on the
principles of poetic art as exemplified by the
poetry of all the great literatures."

Meantime the " principles of poetic art,"
expounded by Watts-Dunton in the *Encyclopædia Britannica,* had attracted the attention
of other editors. Besides the *Examiner,* he
wrote for the *Academy,* and the *English Illus-
trated Magazine.* It was generally recognised
in fact, that had he served an apprenticeship to
literature with the distinct object of reviewing
the chief Victorian poets as their works came
from the Press, he could not have been more
fully equipped than he proved himself to be,
especially when selected to undertake the duties

of leading critic on the *Athenæum*. His connection with that journal extended without
intermission over more than five-and-twenty
years (1876-1902). At one time—more parti-
cularly during the " eighties "—scarcely a week
went by without an article from his pen, reviewing some book of exceptional interest to the
literary world. He reviewed in the *Athenæum*
every book published by Swinburne, in prose as
well as in poetry, for twenty-two years (between
1877 and 1899)—some fifteen volumes in all.
He reviewed every book by William Morris
published between 1888 and 1897—no less than
ten volumes. He reviewed all Tennyson's later
works, a volume of poems by George Meredith,
and a volume of Rossetti's collected works.
He reviewed most of Victor Hugo's publications
between 1877 and 1882 ; and besides all these
critiques, some of them filling five or six columns
of the *Athenæum*, he wrote lengthy reviews on
many of the minor poets, novelists, and essayists
of that mid-Victorian period.

In the writing of these numerous reviews,
it naturally followed that Watts-Dunton's treatise on Poetry came to be gradually absorbed.
It had been freely drawn upon for his essay
in the *Britannica*, as already mentioned ; and

so it came about that the original work in its
manuscript form finally ceased to exist, except
in the pages of the periodicals to which he had
contributed his diverse articles on poetic criticism.

These poetic criticisms, however, were by no
means confined to the literary journals. He
wrote at the request of the editor of *Chambers's
Encyclopædia* the article on the " Sonnet " for
that publication in 1891. Again, there was
his preface to " Chatterton," written for J. H.
Ward's " British Poets " in 1880, prior to the
" Sonnet " essay, it will be noted, and also
prior to the essay on " Poetry " in the *Britannica*. It was while writing on Chatterton, in
fact, that he first struck the keynote to which
all his subsequent essays on Poetry responded.
He regarded that " marvellous boy " as " the
renascence of wonder incarnate "—the poet
who " refused to be imprisoned in the jar of
eighteenth century convention." " Chatterton " was one of his pet subjects ; his favourite
poet, Keats, scarcely won from him greater
admiration. At the time when he was writing
this " Chatterton " preface, it chanced that he
was thrown almost daily into the society of
D. G. Rossetti, whose appreciation of the poet

was, if possible, greater than Watts-Dunton's ; and so deeply interested was Rossetti in the progress of the Chatterton essay, which the author read and re-read to him during their evenings together at Cheyne Walk, that he consulted every work on Chatterton that he could procure in order that he might claim the privilege of tendering his advice when the manuscript was submitted to him for criticism. This criticism on Rossetti's part Watts-Dunton regarded as being extremely valuable, for, as he has recorded in this volume, " the poet of ' Christabel ' himself was scarcely more steeped in the true magic of the romantic temper than was the writer of the " Blessed Damozel " and " Sister Helen."

From this moment the " renascence of wonder " became the central idea in Watts-Dunton's work on Poetry ; and when, in 1904, some twenty years later than the period of his contribution to Ward's " British Poets," Dr. Patrick, the editor of Chambers's *Cyclopædia of English Literature*, asked him to contribute the Introduction to the third volume of that publication, he wrote his now famous essay— scarcely less famous than the " Poetry " essay —known as " The Renascence of Wonder in English Poetry."

Acting as my friend's confidential secretary during the last fifteen years of his life, every opportunity was afforded me of convincing myself that the project of publishing his work on Poetry was never entirely absent from his mind. It was the ruling passion. Other literary projects intervened, projects that appeared to him to demand more immediate attention—those fugitive essays, mostly on poetic subjects, contributed to various journals—and the work on Poetry was put aside, for the moment. But all these interruptions that come to a man of letters who is also engaged in professional duties never tended to damp his ardour.

At last he conceived the idea of seriously preparing his work for the Press, based on his essays on " Poetry and the Renascence of Wonder." The new work, according to the scheme he had begun to devise, was to include selections from his criticisms on Poetry contributed to the *Athenæum*. These selections, he considered, could be appropriately inserted in the shape of riders—" *Athenæum* riders," as he called them—wherever the treatment of the subject would seem to demand elucidation. All the riders that he selected and arranged have now been introduced and printed through-

out the volume in a closer type than the essay
" Poetry " and the essay " The Renascence of
Wonder," which have been reproduced without
any material alteration.

It was, however, it should be mentioned,
through the untiring energy and assistance of
his friend, Mr. Herbert Jenkins, to whom he
consented to entrust the present publication,
that this satisfactory state of things with regard
to the planning of the new work was brought
about. Numerous interviews and a considerable amount of correspondence took place
between author and publisher before the matter
was finally settled. When, however, the agree-
ment came to be signed by Watts-Dunton, in
February, 1914, he appeared to be thoroughly
contented, for he wrote to Mr. Jenkins at the
time, " I can but congratulate myself upon
having found a publisher of the real literary
temper."

During the last few months of his life my
friend was giving nearly all his time to this
volume which he ultimately decided to call
" Poetry and the Renascence of Wonder."
One morning, while turning over the pages of
the manuscript, he said to me, with sudden
elation in his voice, " This book, which I have

always looked upon as my *magnum opus*, is going to be published after all. My greatest aim in life is going to be achieved at last." He had, in fact, put heart and soul into the task he had set himself to accomplish. Nor can there be any doubt that had " Poetry and the Renascence of Wonder " issued from the Press under his personal supervision—had he himself corrected and revised the proof-sheets—the book would have been much fuller, if not as complete as it was originally his ambitious thought to make it. It is only fair to state, moreover, that the method of arrangement— the order, for instance—in which the " *Athenæum* riders " were inserted by him, was merely tentative ; and while adding to these riders, which he had so far selected (and he would undoubtedly have added a large number had he lived) he would have seen to it that every one of them had, throughout the volume, a *raison d'être* in its relation to the context.

Swinburne in his collection of essays, " Studies in Prose and Poetry," has remarked, " The first critic of our time—perhaps the largest minded and surest sighted of any age— has pointed out in an essay on Poetry, which should not be too long buried in the columns

of the *Encyclopædia Britannica*, the exhaustive
accuracy of Greek terms which define every
claimant to the laurel as either a singer or a
maker." Another writer, commenting recently upon this appreciation, has said that,
" After reading Watts-Dunton's essay on Poetry
one will probably think Swinburne's praise not
much beyond the truth. . . By a personal,
an almost emotional quality sometimes to be
found in the best English and French criticism,
it rises from science to the literature of power."

It should be clearly understood, however,
with regard to this volume, that I have
had grave doubts as to the advisability of
inserting the unfinished riders. The difficult
question with which I was confronted
was : Should the essay on " Poetry " and the
essay on " The Renascence of Wonder " be
printed as they appeared respectively in the
Encyclopædia Britannica and the *Cyclopædia of
English Literature*, or should they be issued
with the riders as placed by the author, ten-
tatively, while revising his work ? After
careful deliberation I decided to adopt the
latter course, differentiating between the original
and the added matter in such a way * as to

* The text of the essays as they originally appeared is set with
wider spaces between the lines, whereas the new matter, or riders,
is set " solid," that is, without leads or spaces.

enable the student to read the one, should he prefer it, without taking heed of the other.

Watts-Dunton himself regarded his essay on " Poetry " as it appeared in the *Encyclopædia Britannica* as the basis of his reputation as a critic. And in one of his last remarks on the subject he has recorded what is undeniably true as to the time and thought expended upon the essay ; it seems even to suggest a half-conscious challenge—" Poetry and the Renascence of Wonder," he said, " is the result of years of quiet meditation in the country, and, for good or for ill, absolutely original."

THOMAS HAKE.

CONTENTS

POETRY

POETRY

POETRY

I

IN modern criticism the word poetry is used sometimes to denote any expression (artistic or other) of imaginative feeling, sometimes to designate one of the fine arts.

As an expression of imaginative feeling, as the movement of energy, as one of those great primal human forces which go to the development of the race, poetry in the wide sense has played as important a part as science. In some literatures (such as that of England) poetic energy and in others (such as that of Rome) poetic art is the dominant quality. It is the same with individual writers. In classical literature Pindar may perhaps be taken as a type of the poets of energy ; Virgil of the poets of art. With all his wealth of poetic art Pindar's mastery over symmetrical methods never taught him to " sow with the hand," as Corinna declared, while his poetic energy always impelled him to " sow with the whole sack." In English poetical literature Elizabeth Barrett Browning typifies, perhaps, the poets of energy ; while Keats (notwithstanding all his unquestionable inspiration) is mostly taken as a type of the poets of art. In French literature Hugo, notwithstanding all his mastery over poetic methods, represents the poets of energy. Nature has always been loath, except in cases of her very choicest favourites, to combine true artistic instincts with great poetic energy.

In some writers, and these the very greatest —in Homer, Æschylus, Sophocles, Dante, Shakespeare, Milton, and perhaps Goethe— poetic energy and poetic art are seen in something like equipoise. It is of poetry as an art, however, that we have mainly to speak here ; and all we have to say upon poetry as an energy is that the critic who, like Aristotle, takes this wide view of poetry—the critic who, like him, recognizes the importance of poetry in its relations to man's other expressions of spiritual force, claims a place in point of true critical sagacity above that of a critic who, like Plato, fails to recognise that importance. And assuredly no philosophy of history can be other than inadequate should it ignore the fact that poetry has had as much effect upon human destiny as that other great human energy by aid of which, from the discovery of the use of fire to that of the electric light, the useful arts have been developed.

With regard to poetry as an art, these remarks must be confined to general principles. To treat historically so vast a subject as poetry would be obviously impossible here.

All that can be attempted is to inquire—

(1) What is poetry?

(2) What is the position it takes up in relation to the other arts?

(3) What is its value and degree of expressional power in relation to these? and, finally,

(4) What varieties of poetic art are the outcome of the two great kinds of poetic impulse, dramatic imagination and lyric or egoistic imagination?

II

DEFINITIONS are for the most part alike unsatisfactory and treacherous ; but definitions of poetry are proverbially so. Is it possible to lay down " invariable principles " of poetry, such as those famous " invariable principles " of the Rev. William Lisle Bowles, which in the earlier part of the century awoke the admiration of Southey and the wrath of Byron ? Is it possible for a critic to say of any metrical phrase, stanza, or verse, " This is poetry," or " This is not poetry ? " Can he, with anything like the authority with which the man of science pronounces upon the natural objects brought before him, pronounce upon the qualities of a poem ? These are questions that have engaged the attention of critics ever since the time of Aristotle.

Byron, in his rough and ready way, has answered them in one of those letters to the late John Murray, which, rich as they are in nonsense, are almost as rich in sense. " So far are principles of poetry from being invariable," says he, " that they never were nor ever will be settled. These principles mean nothing more than the predilections of a particular age, and every age has its own and a different one from its predecessor. It is now Homer and now Virgil ; once Dryden and since Sir Walter Scott ; now Corneille and now Racine ; now Crébillon and now Voltaire." This is putting the case very strongly—perhaps too strongly.

It is unquestioned that all artistic criticism is based very largely on sanctions that are in a deep sense conventional. Absolute æsthetics are as impossible as absolute ethics —as impossible as absolute theology ; and beauty itself is entirely a relative term, depending for its acceptance upon the relations existing between the admirer and the object admired, as Darwin has proved. There has been much talk about the glory of peacocks' tails, and we are assured that it took the peacock many thousands of years to develop that gorgeous appendage, which gives the peahen as much joy as the peacock himself, though it does not necessarily follow from this that the peacock's tail is, as a conception, absolutely, universally, and eternally beautiful. That it is beautiful in the eyes of the peahen is as it should be ; but racial prejudice must be taken into account.

To the grub which the peacock will sometimes condescend to devour there is nothing beautiful in that array of feathers which the grub's own juices contribute, however unwillingly, to feed and support. And if the associative origin of beauty is apparent in the natural world, how should it be otherwise in the world of art ? For instance, in the matter of the Venus of Japan and Chelsea there are heretics in regard to her charms, just as in the region of Tottenham Court Road there are said to be good folk, but heretical, who see no loveliness in sage greens.

If we remember that Sophocles lost the first prize for the Œdipus Tyrannus ; if we remember what in Dante's time (owing partly, no doubt, to the universal ignorance of Greek) were the relative positions of Homer and Virgil, what in the time of Milton were the relative positions of Milton himself, of Shakespeare, and of Beaumont and Fletcher ; again if we remember Jeffrey's famous classification of the poets of his day, we shall be driven to pause over Byron's words before dismissing them. Yet some definition, for the purpose of this essay, must be here attempted ; and, using the phrase " absolute poetry " as the musical critics use the phrase " absolute music," we may, perhaps, without too great presumption submit the following :—

Absolute poetry is the concrete and artistic ex-

pression of the human mind in emotional and rhythmical language.

This at least will be granted, that no literary expression can properly speaking be called poetry that is not in a certain deep sense emotional, whatever may be its subject matter, concrete in its method and its diction, rhythmical in movement, and artistic in form.

That the expression of all real poetry must be concrete in method and diction is obvious, and yet this dictum would exclude from the definition much of what is called didactic poetry. With abstractions the poet has nothing to do, save to take them and turn them into concretions ; for, as artist, he is simply the man who by instinct embodies in concrete forms that " universal idea " which Gravina speaks of— that which is essential and elemental in nature and in man ; as poetic artist he is simply the man who by instinct chooses for his concrete forms metrical language. And the questions to be asked concerning any work of art are simply these—

Is that which is here embodied really permanent, universal, and elemental ? And is the concrete form embodying it really beautiful— acknowledged as beautiful by the soul of man

in its highest moods ?   Any other question is
an impertinence.

Examples are always useful in discussions
such as this.

As an example of the absence of concrete form
in verse take the following lines from George
Eliot's Spanish Gipsy :—

> " Speech is but broken light upon the depth
> Of the unspoken ; even your loved words
> Float in the larger meaning of your voice
> As something dimmer."

Without discussing the question of blank
verse cadence and the weakness of a line where
the main accent falls upon a positive hiatus,
" of the unspoken," we would point out that
this powerful passage shows the spirit of poetry
without its concrete form.   The abstract method
is substituted for the concrete.   Such an abstract
phrase as " the unspoken " belongs entirely to
prose.

Matthew Arnold defined poetry as a " criticism of life."   If by this is meant that poetry
is the result of a criticism of life ; that just as
the poet's metrical effects are and must be the
result of a thousand semi-conscious generalizations upon the laws of cause and effect in metric
art, so the beautiful things he says about life,
and the beautiful pictures he paints of life, are
the result of his generalizations upon life as he

passes through it ; and consequently that the value of his poetry consists in the beauty and the truth of his generalizations.

There is, of course, little to be said against this.

Yet, it must be confessed, so dangerous is it to indulge in formulas that, having decided that poetry consists of generalizations on human life, Arnold in reading poetry keeps on the watch for those generalizations, and has really at last learned to think that the less they are hidden behind the dramatic action, the more unmistake-ably they are intended as generalizations, the better.

As to what is called ratiocinative poetry, it might perhaps be shown that it does not exist at all. Not by syllogism, but per saltum must the poet reach in every case his conclusions. We listen to the poet—we allow him to address us in rhythm or in rhyme—we allow him to sing to us while other men are only allowed to talk, not because he argues more logically than they, but because he feels more deeply and perhaps more truly. It is for his listeners to be knowing and ratiocinative ; it is for him to be gnomic and divinely wise.

That poetry must be metrical or even rhyth-mical in movement, however, is what some have denied. Here we touch at once the very root of the subject. The difference between all literature and mere " word-kneading " is that, while literature is alive, word-kneading is without life. This literary life, while it is only bipartite in prose, seems to be tripartite in poetry ; that is to say, while prose requires intellectual life and emotional life, poetry seems to require not only intellectual life and emotional life, but rhythmic life, this last being the most important of all according to many critics, though Aristotle is not among these. Here indeed is the " fork " between the old critics and the new. Unless the rhythm of any metrical passage is so vigorous, so natural, and so free that it seems as though it could live, if need were, by its rhythm alone, has that passage any right to exist ? and should it not, if the substance is good, be forthwith demetricized and turned into prose ? Thoreau has affirmed that prose at its best, has high qualities of its own beyond the ken of poetry ; to compensate for the sacrifice of these should not the metrical gains of any passage be beyond all cavil ?

But this argument might be pressed further still. It might seem bold to assert that, in many cases, the mental value of poetry may actually depend upon form and colour, but would it not be true ? The mental value of poetry must be

judged by a standard not applicable to prose ;
but, even with regard to the different kinds of
poetry we must not compare poetry whose
mental value consists in a distinct and logical
enunciation of ideas, such as that of Lucretius
and Wordsworth, and poetry whose mental
value consists partly in the suggestive richness
of passion or symbol latent in rhythm (such as
that of Sappho sometimes, Pindar often, Shelley
always), or latent in colour, such as that of
some of the Persian poets. To discuss the question, Which of these two kinds of poetry is more
precious ? would be idle, but are we not
driven to admit that certain poems whose
strength is rhythm and certain other poems
whose strength is colour, while devoid of any
logical statement of thought, may be as fruitful
of thoughts and emotions too deep for words
as a shaken prism is fruitful of tinted lights ?
The mental forces at work in the production of
a poem like the Excursion are of a very different
kind from the mental forces at work in the
production of a poem like Shelley's " Ode to
the West Wind." In the one case the poet's
artistic methods, like those of the Greek architects, show, and are intended to show, the solid
strength of the structure. In the other, the

poet's artistic methods like those of the Arabian
architect contradict the idea of solid strength
—make the structure appear to hang over our
heads like the cloud pageantry of heaven. But,
in both cases, the solid strength is, and must be,
there, at the base. Before the poet begins to
write he should ask himself which of these
artistic methods is natural to him ; he should
ask himself whether his natural impulse is towards the weighty iambic movement whose
primary function is to state, or towards those
lighter movements which we still call, for want
of more convenient words, anapæstic and
dactylic, whose primary function is to suggest.
Nor is it difficult to see why English anapæstic
and dactylic verse must suggest and not
state, as even so comparatively successful
a *tour de force* as Shelley's " Sensitive Plant "
shows. Conciseness is a primary virtue of all
statement. The moment the English poet tries
to " pack " his anapæstic or dactylic line, as
he can pack his iambic line, his versification
becomes rugged, harsh, pebbly—becomes so of
necessity. Nor is this all ; anapæstic and dactylic
verse must in English be obtrusively alliterative,
or the same pebbly effect begins to be felt. The
anapæstic line is so full of syllables that in a

language where the consonants dominate the vowels (as in English), these syllables grate against each other, unless their corners are artfully bevelled by one of the only two smoothing processes at the command of an English versifier—obtrusive alliteration, or an obtrusive use of liquids. Now these demands of form may be turned by the perfect artist to good account if his appeal to the listener's soul is primarily that of suggestion by sound or symbol, but if his appeal is that of direct and logical statement the diffuseness inseparable from good anapæstic and dactylic verse is a source of weakness such as the true artist should find intolerable.

English poets, perhaps, may be divided into born rhymers to whom rhyme is a spur, and those to whom rhyme is not a spur but a curb ; and the two kinds of poets are curiously exemplified in the joint authors of Lyrical Ballads, Wordsworth and Coleridge. It may almost be said that Coleridge thought in rhyme, and that he never adequately expressed himself except in rhyme : certainly it may be said that it was only in rhyme that he achieved his crowning quality of Naïveté. His rhyme facilities are infinite. Every kind of rhyme-effect was at his command. Take, for instance, rhyme sinphasis. In the Ancient Mariner he made it his paramount endeavour to be emphatic and

understood at first sight. From a letter of the
late Rev. Alexander Dyce to the late H.N.
Coleridge, we learn what was the inception of
the story of the "Ancient Mariner." This was
not the incident of the albatross in Shelvock's
voyages, as is commonly supposed, but a dream
of a phantom "skeleton ship with figures in it,"
related to Coleridge by a friend. Now when
Coleridge proceeded to write this poem his
object was to produce the most vivid poetical
narrative of his time—to give as unmistakeable
a picture as possible of a phantom "skeleton
ship with figures in it." The incident of the
albatross was only used to furnish a cause for
the appearance of the phantom ship, and for the
location of its appearance. From the first line
of the poem to the actual appearance of the
phantom ship on the horizon, everything is
made to yield, when necessary to this end.
The most effective way of depicting the "skeleton ship with figures in it" was, of course, to
place it between the spectator and the sinking
sun, which would then shine through its ghastly
skeleton ribs. In order to do this, the sun and
the phantom ship must be painted in very
strong colour at whatsoever sacrifice of grace,
and as the rhyme-word is always ten times
stronger than any other word, "Sun" must be
the rhyme-word.

Accordingly Coleridge paints the picture by
daring rhymed-tautology such as an inferior poet
would shrink from. He knew that tautology
in its proper place is a legitimate implement in
the hands of a poet, and that the dread of using

it is one of the surest signs of timid mediocrity.

> See! See! (I cried) she tacks no more!
>   Hither to work us weal—
> Without a breeze, without a tide,
>   Steadies with upright keel!
>
> The western wave was all aflame;
>   The day was well-nigh done!
> Almost upon the western wave
>   Rested the broad, bright sun,
> When that strange ship drove suddenly
>   Betwixt us and the sun.
>
> And straight the sun was flecked with bars
>   (Heaven's mother send us grace)
> As if through a dungeon grate he peered
>   With broad and burning face.

Here the poet not only repeats the phrase "western wave," but repeats "Sun" as a rhyme-word.

He realized more fully than did any other English poet the fact that every poem has, like a piece of tapestry, its inner side (the poet's own), and its outer side (the reader's), and that while the perfect master of poetry-weaving works so that his pattern is developed on the outside (the reader's side) the imperfect artist, such as Donne or Browning, is apt to work in the contrary way—so that while he himself sees the pattern from within, the outer surface presents the reader with the tangles and knots of many-coloured worsted which should be seen by the poet-weaver alone. That the weaver pleases himself hugely by thus keeping the picture for himself and presenting the knots and tangles to the spectator is obvious, and perhaps it is, after all, worth while to weave one's tapestry for one's own delectation. But then the weaver-poet is never content with this. He weaves not, like the bower bird, for himself and his mate, but for the outer world, and to surpass all other bower birds in the art of weaving.

To the perfect poetic artist it is not a trouble, but a delight, to be continually transplanting himself to the reader's outer standpoint by a rapid kind of imaginative process, the effect of which is similar to that of the little mirrors which the tapestry-weavers hang before their work to show them how the pattern is being developed on the right side of the stuff. Yet Coleridge's critical knowledge of his art was as wonderful as his instinctive mastery over it. The rhyme principle of modern Europe may be answerable in a large degree for that romantic luxury and apparent lawlessness of methods which have been so often contrasted with the purity of the classic style. The moment a born-rhymer has chosen a word for the end of a line all the feasible rhymes in the language leap into his brain like sparks from a rocket. Some poets by instinct take the first spark that rises, and use its suggestions ; others by instinct wait and select. In reading any poet it is perfectly easy to see to which class he belongs. In the heat of composition the sudden inquiry for a rhyme will call up a long-forgotten suggestion or thought or emotion which, though perhaps partially in harmony with the situation, is only partially so, and then sore is the rhymer's temptation to go astray.

Although at first the feeble relevancy of the image suggested by rhyme may be apparent enough to the rhymer's judgment, it must be dismissed firmly, and at once, or disasters will follow ; for in art, as in common life, it is aston- ishing how soon the judgment will yield to any one of the other faculties, such as fancy, imagina- tion, etc.

In discarding the incongruous or only partially congruous fancy suggested by rhyme the rhymer who hesitates is lost. To dally with it is to be- come familiar with it, and to become familiar with it is in most cases to begin to love it, and then its rejection becomes impossible.

The richer the mind of any poet, the more multitudinous and the more clamorous are the " thick-coming fancies " suggested by each im- pact of the outer world upon the poet's soul.

In proportion to the activity of the eyes that see is the difficulty of shutting in the one object which alone should be seen. This, indeed, is apparent not in modern literature only ; we see it even among the Greek poets, whose vehicle —rhymeless and quantitative—was so flexible that the poetic vision was probably disturbed in only a slight degree by the demands of form ; for those who talk so much about the severity of the Greek note are apt to think too much of Sophocles, and too little of Æschylus and Pindar.

But with regard to modern poetry this is doubtless why such overloaded narratives as

'Venus and Adonis' and 'Endymion' (where the demands of narrative art are completely ignored) came to be written by two poets, one of whom was actually, and the other potentially among the greatest that have appeared in England.

The fact is that no two poets ever did work alike. It is when we contrast Coleridge's style with Wordsworth's, and the methods by which the two styles are reached, that we see how infinite in variety is the form of expression of every faculty and endowment of man.

Wordsworth's tinkering of his sonnet "Toussaint l'ouverture" actually recasting it several times made Rossetti say that he was no poet at all. It simply proves, however, that the poet, having made first a rigorous selection of the line-ending word, and then again a rigorous selection of the answering rhyme-word, filled up the line with unripe material, which became afterwards poetized by the mellowing sun of his genius.

Keats's work, like Swinburne's, shows the very opposite of this method—it shows that simultaneously with the rhyme selection comes a line of ripe and almost perfectly poetized material. With each poet the method adopted is, as we have hinted, a matter of temperament, not of consciousness, perhaps, and certainly not of volition, and both methods have their advantages—both their disadvantages.

A poet like Keats and a poet like Swinburne, who in this matter alone resemble each other, with the entire poetic diction of our literature

at their fingers' ends, and an enormous poetical
diction of their own invention to boot, have no
need to subject their lines to the poetizing
process of Wordsworth, for as regards poetic
material they find every rhyme-word as luminous
of tail as a comet, as is only too clearly seen in
' Endymion ' and in some of Swinburne's
poems.

But then, for this very reason, they have no
time to consider selection and economy, and it
is obvious that without a great deal of rhyme
selection the climacteric goal of the poem must
needs be reached but slowly and circuitously.
For not merely every drama, but every poetical
work from the epic to the sonnet or roundel,
has its climacteric goal, which has to be reached
in the most economical way according to the
methods of the form of art adopted.

It is, of course, in the nature of things that
poems in which there has been a too rigorous
selection of rhymes, as is often the case with
Tennyson, are apt to fail in inspiration, while
poems in which there has been a too hurried
selection of rhymes, as with Keats and Swinburne, sometimes lack that concentration which
characterizes the perfect work of the greatest
masters.

In English rhymed measures in which the
paucity of rhyme is so troublesome, it may
almost be affirmed that the thing said is a third
something between the idea and the rhyme. A
notable instance of this occurs in the conclusion
of Keats's "The Eve of St. Agnes," which it will
be remembered runs thus :—

> " And they are gone ; ay, ages long ago
>   These lovers fled away into the storm.
> That night the Baron dreamt of many a woe,
>   And all his warrior-guests, with shade and form
>   Of witch, and demon, and large coffin-worm,
> Were long be-nightmared. Angela the old
>   Died palsy-twitch'd, with meagre face deform ;
> The Beadsman, after thousand aves told,
> For aye unsought-for slept among his ashes cold."

Now, if we consider how fantastic (according to the law of association of ideas) are the conceptions of " Coffin-worm " and " Angela's meagre face deform " in relation to the elopement of two lovers, and if we also recollect how few are the available rhymes to the initial rhyme-word " storm," we shall see that it was mainly rhyme-necessity which caused the warriors to dream of " Coffin-worm " and mainly rhyme-necessity which caused poor Angela (who deserved " to die on a feather-bed sipping a cup of spiced wine ") to have such a miserable latter end going off " palsy-twitched," with meagre face deform."

It is true that a revered student of Keats has tried to explain away the poet's yielding to rhyme suggestion here, but I fear without avail or merit whatever. But suppose that before he sat down to write ' Endymion ' Keats had studied this important matter of rhyme-selection—that he had learnt that a rigid rhyme-selection is one of the first requisites of rhymed-poetry—what an ' Endymion ' he might have given us then !

For ever since the infamous attacks in Blackwood's and the Quarterly upon ' Endymion ' the fashion has survived of underestimating the marvellous poem. It is crammed full of poetry.

In the end Keats did learn all this, no doubt, for deficient as " Lamia " is in spirituality from the romantic point of view its strength and masculine grip are very largely the result of effective rhyme-selection. And as for the great odes—the most perfect work, from the artist's point of view, that was produced in England in the last century—they could never have existed at all without it.

But if the importance of metrical effects is seen in rhymed-poetry, how much more strongly are they seen in English blank verse in which so much of our great English poetry is embodied. Here the critic's outlook is so widespread and so various that he may well stand aghast before it. It is the most difficult of all movements, and yet it seems the easiest.

There seems to be a fatality about the writing of English blank verse. The fundamental difference between rhymed verse and blank verse is that while rhymed verse has for support harmony, melody, rhyme, and colour, and can in the level and working passages of a poem dispense with mere elevation of style, blank verse, though it has all these save rhyme, cannot without elevation of style exist at all ; and if the mere working portions of a poem are too level in matter to call up the glow requisite to give this elevation, an artificial elevation has to be manufactured for blank verse to distinguish it from prose. Moreover, as in other matters of elevation or individual accent, the poet's style

is sure to reach its culmination, and then it is
liable to degenerate at once into mere manner
—afterwards to sink farther still into mannerism.
The poet begins by modelling his style upon
that of previous writers, or a previous writer—
strikes out at last a style of his own, works in it,
elaborates it, brings it to perfection, and then
overdoes it. Shakespeare is an illustrious example of this. He began by imitating Marlowe,
but finding (what most likely Marlowe would
have found had he lived) that the " mighty
line " is quite unfitted to render the varied
fluctuant life of drama (being really an epic
movement), he invented a style of his own.
The miracle of this later style is that the pleasure
we get from it is a something between the
pleasure afforded by perfect prose rhythm and
the pleasure afforded by poetic rhythm.

And when we consider that the pleasure
afforded by poetic rhythm is that of expecting
the fulfilment of a recognized law of cadence,
while the pleasure afforded by prose rhythm is
that its cadences shall come upon us by surprise,
it is no wonder if Shakespeare is the only poet
who can catch and secure both these kinds of
pleasure and alternate them.

But even Shakespeare was human, the older
he got and the more he drank the delight of
faithfully rendering Nature, the more he felt
inclined to make the expected cadence (the
cadence of art) yield to the unexpected cadence
(that of nature) ; and in some of his latest plays
there are often between the great passages
tracts of matter which, so far as any *metrical*

music goes, might as well have been written in prose.

And in the same way Milton, beginning also with Marlowe's movement, carrying it to its highest possible point in the early books of " Paradise Lost," could hardly finish the poem without being overmastered by the style natural to his own didactic instincts, which in " Paradise Regained " flattened the lines and produced his mannerism.

In the ' 'Morte d'Arthur " Tennyson had reached a style exceedingly noble of its kind, it seemed to combine the excellencies of Wordsworth and of Milton. And the blank verse of " Guinevere " was also very fine, though there were unpleasant affectations—such obvious tricks, for instance, as that of seeking perpetually to get emphasis by throwing a long pause after the first foot of the line, a device which Milton had already made so stale that it is surprising any successor dared to venture upon it. But from the publication of " Guinevere " Tennyson's style stiffened with every poem, became more mannered and more cold.

Stiffness in blank verse arises from an attempt to hold up artificially sentences by forcing into them parenthetical matter, and so producing an artificial elevation, instead of suffering no sentence to be elevated save by the only natural means of elevation—that of the thought or emotion which gives the sentence birth.

Of course, no subject is fit for treatment in blank verse unless it can call from the writer sufficient glow of emotion to raise it to, and sustain it at, the elevation required for cadence without any resort to artifices such as that of parenthetical interpolation or antithetical balancing.

But enough has been said to show that in discussing poetry questions of versification touch, as we have said, the very root of the subject.

Using the word " form " in a wider sense still, a sense that includes " composition," it can be shown that poetry to be entitled to the name must be artistic in form. Whether a poem be a Welsh triban or a stornello improvised by an Italian peasant girl, whether it be an ode by Keats or a tragedy by Sophocles, it is equally a work of art. The artist's command over form may be shown in the peasant girl's power of spontaneously rendering in simple verse, in her stornello or rispetto, her emotions through nature's symbols ; it may be shown by Keats in that perfect fusion of all poetic elements of which he was such a master, in the manipulation of language so beautiful both for form and colour that thought and words seem but one blended loveliness ; or it may be shown by Sophocles in a mastery over what in painting is called composition, in the exercise of that wise vision of the artist, which, looking before and after, sees the thing of beauty as a whole, and enables him to grasp the eternal laws of cause and effect in art and bend them to his own wizard will. In every case, indeed, form is an essential part of poétry ; and, although George Sand's saying that " L'art n'est qu' une forme " applies perhaps more strictly to the plastic arts (where the soul is reached partly through mechanical means), its application to poetry can hardly be exaggerated.

Owing, however, to the fact that the word ποιητής (first used to designate the poetic artist by Herodotus) means maker, Aristotle seems to have assumed that the indispensable basis of poetry is invention. He appears to have thought that a poet is a poet more on account of the composition of the action than on account of the composition of his verses. Indeed he said as much as this. Of epic poetry he declared emphatically that it produces its imitations either by mere articulate words or by metre super-added. This is to widen the definition of poetry so as to include all imaginative literature, and Plato seems to have given an equally wide meaning to the word ποιησις. Only, while Aristotle considered ποιησις to be an imitation of the facts of nature, Plato considered it to be an imitation of the dreams of man. Aristotle ignored, and Plato slighted, the importance of versification (though Plato on one occasion admitted that he who did not know rhythm could be called neither musician or poet).

It is impossible to discuss here the question whether an imaginative work in which the method is entirely concrete and the expression entirely emotional, while the form is unmetrical, is or is not entitled to be called a poem. That there may be a kind of unmetrical narrative so poetic in motive, so concrete in diction, so emotional in treatment, as to escape altogether from those critical canons usually applied to prose, we shall see when, in discussing the epic, we come to touch upon the Northern sagas.

Perhaps the first critic who tacitly revolted against the dictum that substance, and not form, is the indispensable basis of poetry was Dionysius of Halicarnassus, whose treatise upon the arrangement of words is really a very fine piece of literary criticism. In his acute remarks upon the arrangement of the words in the sixteenth book of the Odyssey, as compared with that in the story of Gyges by Herodotus, was perhaps first enunciated clearly the doctrine that poetry is fundamentally a matter of style. The Aristotelian theory as to invention, however, dominated all criticism after as well as before Dionysius. When Bacon came to discuss the subject (and afterwards) the only division between the poetical critics was perhaps between the followers of Aristotle and those of Plato as to what poetry should, and what it should not, imitate. It is curious to speculate as to what would have been the result had the poets followed the critics in this matter. Had not the instinct of the poet been too strong for the schools, would poetry as an art have been lost and merged in such imaginative prose as Plato's ? Or is not the instinct for form too strong to be stifled ?

By the poets themselves metre was always considered to be the one indispensable requisite of a poem, though, as regards criticism, so recently as the time of the appearance of the Waverley Novels, the Quarterly Review would sometimes speak of them as " poems " ; and perhaps even now there are critics of a very high rank who would do the same with regard to romances so concrete in method and diction, and so full of poetic energy, as Wuthering Heights and Jane Eyre, where we get absolutely all that Aristotle requires for a poem. On the whole, however, the theory that versification is not an indispensable requisite of a poem seems to have become nearly obsolete in our time. Perhaps, indeed, many critics would now go so far in the contrary direction as to say with Hegel (Aesthetik, iii. p. 289) that " metre is the first and only condition absolutely demanded by poetry, yea even more necessary than a figurative picturesque diction." At all events this at least may be said that in our own time the division between poetical critics is not between Aristotelians and Baconians ; it is now of a different kind altogether.

While one group of critics may still perhaps say with Dryden that " a poet is a maker, as the name signifies," and that " he who cannot make, that is, invent, has his name for nothing," another group contends that it is not the invention but the artistic treatment, the form, which determines whether an imaginative writer is a poet or a writer of prose—contends in short, that emotion is the basis of all true poetic expression, whatever be the subject matter, that thoughts must be expressed in an emotional manner before they can be brought into poetry, and that this emotive expression demands even yet something else, viz., style and form,

But, although, many critics are now agreed that " L'art n'est qu' une forme," that without metre and without form there can be no poetry, there are few who would contend that poetry can exist by virtue of any of these alone, or even by virtue of all these combined. Quite independent of verbal melody, though mostly accompanying it, and quite independent of " composition," there is an atmosphere floating around the poet through which he sees everything, an atmosphere which stamps his utterances as poetry : for instance, among all the versifiers contemporary with Donne there was none so rugged as he occasionally was, and yet such songs as " Sweetest love, I do not go for weariness of thee " prove how true a poet he was whenever he could succeed in presenting to the reader the right side of the tapestry that he was weaving. While rhythm may to a very considerable degree be acquired (though, of course, the highest rhythmical effects never can), the power of looking at the world through the atmosphere that floats before the poet's eyes is not to be learned and not to be taught. This atmosphere is what we call *poetic imagination*, an atmosphere which, while it transfigures and ennobles human life, gives it also a certain quality which may perhaps be called a dignified remoteness. What the artistic poet gains in dignity, however, he loses in other ways. As a witness of the human drama, for instance, he loses in apparent trust-worthiness and apparent authority. " The light that never was on sea or land " is apt to fall with a somewhat chilling effect upon this our real land where men and women live and love and hate and strive. There is one poet, however, whose muse knew no such light—Robert Browning. He gazed at the world through no atmosphere of the golden clime, but confronted life with the frank familiar eyes with which the actors in the real drama gaze at each other. This lends his work a freshness peculiar to itself, but gives it also that air of familiarity which is perhaps the proper quest of the prose delineator of human life rather than that of the poet, a subject which will have to be fully discussed further on. But first it seems necessary to say a word or two upon that high temper of the soul which in truly great poetry gives birth to this poetic imagination.

The " Message " of poetry must be more unequivocal, more thoroughly accentuated, than that of any of the other fine arts. With regard to modern poetry, indeed, it may almost be said that if any writer's verse embodies a message, true, direct, and pathetic, we in modern Europe cannot stay to inquire too curiously about the degree of artistic perfection with which it is delivered, for Wordsworth's saying " That which comes from the heart goes to the heart," applies very closely indeed to modern poetry. The most truly passionate poet in Greece was no doubt in a deep sense the most artistic poet ; but in her case art and passion were one, and that is why she has been so cruelly misunderstood. The most truly passionate nature, and perhaps the greatest soul, that in our time has expressed itself in English verse is Elizabeth Barrett Browning, at least it is certain that, with the single exception of Hood in the " Song of the Shirt," no writer of the nineteenth century has really touched our hearts with a hand so powerful as hers—and this notwithstanding violations of poetic form, notwithstanding defective rhymes, such as would appal some of the contemporary versifiers of England and France " who lisp in numbers for the numbers [and nothing else] come." The truth is that in order to produce poetry the soul must for the time being have reached that state of exultation, that state of freedom from self-consciousness, depicted in the lines :—

" I started once, or seemed to start, in pain,
   Resolved on noble things, and strove to speak,
 As when a great thought strikes along the brain,
   And flushes all the cheek."

Whatsoever may be the poet's " knowledge of his art," into this mood he must always pass before he can write a line of high poetry. For, notwithstanding all that we have said and are going to say upon poetry as a fine art, it is in the deepest sense of the word an " inspiration " indeed. No man can write a line of genuine poetry without having been " born again " (or, as the true rendering of the text says, " born from above ") ; and then the mastery over those highest reaches of form which are beyond the ken of the mere versifier comes to him as a result of the change. Hence, with all Mrs. Browning's metrical blemishes, the splendour of her metrical triumphs at her best [remains].

What is the deep distinction between poet and proseman ? A writer may be many things besides a poet ; he may be a warrior like Æschylus, a man of business like Shakespeare, a courtier like Chaucer, or a cosmopolitan philosopher like Goethe ; but the moment the poetic mood is upon him all the trappings of the world with which for years he may perhaps have been clothing his soul—the world's knowingness, its cynicism, its self-seeking, its ambition —fall away, and the man becomes an inspired child again, with ears attuned to nothing but

the whispers of those spirits from the Golden
Age, who, according to Hesiod, haunt and bless
the degenerate earth.   What such a man
produces may greatly delight and astonish his
readers, yet not so greatly as it delights and
astonishes himself. His passages of pathos draw
no tears so deep or so sweet as those that fall
from his own eyes while he writes ; his sublime
passages overawe no soul so imperiously as his
own ; his humour draws no laughter so rich or
so deep as that stirred within his own breast.

It might almost be said, indeed, that Sincerity and Conscience, the two angels that
bring to the poet the wonders of the poetic
dream, bring him also the deepest, truest delight
of form. It might also be said that by aid of
sincerity and conscience the poet is enabled to
see more clearly than other men the eternal
limits of his own art—to see with Sophocles
that nothing, not even poetry itself, is of any
worth to man, invested as he is by the whole
army of evil, unless it is in the deepest and
highest sense good, unless it comes linking us
all together by closer bonds of sympathy and
pity, strengthening us to fight the foes with
whom fate and even nature, the mother who
bore us, sometimes seem in league—to see with

Milton that the high quality of man's soul which in English is expressed by the word virtue is greater than even the great poem he prized, greater than all the rhythms of all the tongues that have been spoken since Babel—and to see with Shakespeare and with Shelley that the high passion which in English is called love is lovelier than all art, lovelier than all the marble Mercuries that " await the chisel of the sculptor " in all the marble hills.

A poet must indeed feel with Coleridge that poetry is its own exceeding great reward. Like Keats—he must seek the smiles of the mother of Hermes :

> " Seek as they once were sought in Grecian isles,
> By bards who died content on pleasant sward,
> Leaving great verse unto a little clan."

And for this reason in all English poetry, at least, a sense of difficulty overcome must be carefully avoided. Such a feeling destroys it at once as a sincere utterance of the poet's soul. In the poetry of England, we reiterate, so imperative is it that there should be no faintest suspicion of difficulty overcome the moment the singer passes into the true poetic mood, to avoid such a suspicion is the first care with all true poets. So great is the importance of the art of concealing art in high poetry that when the imagination or the heart of the reader is to be touched, there is actually a kind of danger in using any metres save those of the simplest kind. And this, we may be sure, was all that Coleridge meant when he affirmed that the more purely imaginative is the substance of any poem, the simpler must be its method of presentment. As instances of simplicity of form we can point not only to the stanza of the Border ballads, and to such poems as " Laodamia," " Dion," " The Leech Gatherer," " Gray's Elegy," " The Burial of Sir John Moore," and " The Song of the Shirt," but also to such poems in another kind as " The Ancient Mariner," " Christabel," " Sister Helen," " Rose Mary," " Rizpah," &c. And on the other hand we might point to the " Raven," of Edgar Poe, where the poet, though nearly as full of imaginative music as they who wrote the above poems, and quite as eager as they to touch the heart, entangles his strength in the complexities of a form so artificial that even the simplicity of the diction could hardly warm it into true, passionate life. For when Poe himself declared, in criticizing his own poem, that in the expression of passion there is always something of the homely, he would have done better by saying that, although in poetry of deep passion the diction can either be homely or otherwise, what must always be homely is the metrical form.

A very notable instance of the mistake of using elaborately artificial metres for the rendering of simple subjects is afforded by Mistral in his Miréio—a poem in its motive having all the simple charm of Wordsworth, and William Barnes combined. In a lyrical metre of the

most elaborate kind, he describes and tells the
story of the Provençal maid Miréio gathering the
mulberry leaves for her silk-worms, the picture
of the footrace at Nismes, the mowers, the
female hay-makers, the hay-making, the wag-
goners, the treading out of the corn, the lovers
climbing the trees, the nest of the titmice, the
collector of snails, the girls carrying the orange
baskets on head or hip and laughing as they go,
the mirage, Miréio's crossing of the Rhone in
Adrelon's skiff, the girl's sunstroke and swoon
on the banks of the pool, her recall to life by the
mosquitoes—every incident of which is delightful, because it is so fresh and so new. This
makes the special feature of Mirèio the sharp
and perpetual contrast it exhibits between
matter and form.

Turning to English poetry, far more powerful,
and far more enduring than nine-tenths of the
verse of our time, is "Auld Robin Gray"
written in the simplest of all measures. The
same may be said of Emily Brontë's finest poem.
In face of such a poem as Hood's "Bridge of
Sighs" it might, perhaps, seem rash to say that
to English poems of deep pathos monosyllabic
rhymes are essential, and yet we are by no
means sure that this might not be maintained.

For no one will deny that the motive of the
"Bridge of Sighs," is as heart-stirring as the
motive of the "Song of the Shirt," and yet no
one will affirm that the two poems stir the
heart with equal power. It is because anything
that disturbs in the smallest degree the accent
of sincerity is dangerous, is indeed fatal, that in

English lyrics difficult metres are only good when the complexity of the form seems to be disconnected with ingenuity—seems, in a word, to be the result not of metric skill at all, but of the very movement of the poet's passion, as in Shelley's " Skylark," where the poet, listening in a rapt mood to the music of the bird has passed into a temper so exalted that he must needs attune his words to the very accent of the bird himself.

The great law of poetic art, that the more earnest, or impassioned, or imaginative the subject, the more carefully must the mere tricks of the trade be avoided, is not a law invented by man, but is founded on the laws of nature.

Lest any note of self-consciousness should mar the poem's general tone of sincereity, even the commonest resources of the metricist—such, for instance, as that of smoothing the run of the lines by alliteration—have to be disguised, and by instinct are disguised, the moment the poet has passed into the true poetic dream.

Though there are certain kinds of poetry where the smoothing of the lines may be effected by the most primitive kind of alliteration, where the alliterative syllables may run off in couples, or at least the bars of the verse may be marked off by clearly accentuated alliterative syllables, the moment the poet gets into an impassioned mood this is no longer practicable.

The alliterative syllable must, if possible, be embedded in the middle of a word lest serious poetry—which, though an art, is primarily a message—should be degraded by tricks of artifice. So conscious of the supreme import-ance of sincerity was the great master of the lyric of simple passion, Burns, that in one of his songs he actually exchanged a perfect for a less perfect rhyme, as he tells us, merely in order that the song might have the effect, by its artistic deficiency, of being the natural, spon-taneous expression of feeling.

Perhaps it might be too bold to say of Mrs. Browning, the most impassioned of all British poets since Burns, that in the " Cry of the Children," and in some other of her superb lyrics, she on occasion consciously allowed her rhymes to run loose in order to add to the effect of spontaneity, but certainly the imperfect rhyming does sometimes seem to have this effect.

But we must not forget here the obvious division of poetry into worldly and unworldly verse. Indeed, unless we do so divide it, we cannot treat at all of eighteenth century poetry, nor can we treat of nineteenth century poetry as exemplified in the poetry of Byron, whose worldly verse is alone of any great importance among his writings. Among the many functions of poetic art is that of poetising didactic, that is to say prosaic, matter, and bringing it into poetry. For this purpose each literature and each age has had its favourite form.

As the mind of man widens in mere know-ledge and intelligence fresh prose material is being furnished for the poetic laboratory every day. And the question, What is the poetic form best suited to embody and secure this ever-increasing and ever-varying wealth ?—a question which has to be answered by each literature, and indeed by each period of each literature, for itself—goes to the root of poetic criticism. It can of course only be exercised by passing the didactic matter through a laboratory as creative and as recreative as nature's own, the laboratory of a true poet's imagination.

Of course, before didactic matter can become anything more than versified prose, it has to be excarnated from the prose tissue in which all such matter takes birth, and then incarnated anew in the spiritualised tissue of which the poetic body is and must always be composed. Hence it is not enough for the poet to " use the sieve," as Dante would say, in selecting " noble-words." The best prose writers from Plato downwards have been in the habit of doing this. When Waller said :

> Things of deep sense we may in prose unfold,
> But they move more in lofty numbers told—

he meant by " lofty numbers " those semi-poetic " numbers " of the English couplet in which poetised didactics were in his time embodied—as in the time of Shakespeare such poetised secretions of the mere *intellectus cogitabundus* were put into the mouths of dramatic characters, and in the Greek drama they were put for the most part into the mouth of the chorus.

Since the Romantic revival, however, poetic

art has undergone an entire change. Acted drama cannot now receive poetised didactics, which would in these days slacken the movement and disturb the illusion required, while as to the kind of epigram-in-solution or half-poetised quintessential prose which is embodied in the eighteenth-century couplet the criticism of the Romantic revival is apt to consider this not so much as poetry as an intermediate form —and an extremely rich and precious one— between poetry and prose.   Epigrammatic matter must to exist at all, be knowing, and as knowingness and high poetry are mutually destructive, it is evident that some form other than the couplet, which is so associated with epigram, must since the romantic revival be used for the poetising of didactic matter of the unworldly and lofty kind. The form which in the nineteenth century this poetic work has achieved is the sonnet which we shall discuss somewhat fully further on.

Indeed, it is an open question whether since the Romantic revival the sonnet especially as used by Wordsworth has not been gradually taking precedence of most other forms as an embodiment of poetised didactics. And should this on inquiry be found to be the case, the importance of this form will be made manifest.

And this brings us to the interesting question of poetic realism. How much of that dramatic realism of which prose seems to be the natural medium can a poet—without neglecting the demands of poetic art—import into his verses ? Without going so far as to say that according

to the measure of his success in this most
difficult poetic effort is the measure of the
lasting vitality latent in any poet's verses other
than verses of high and impassioned song, we
may at least affirm that those poets of the world
whose measure of success herein has been
greatest are such poets as Homer, Dante, and
Shakespeare. And as to unbeautiful subjects,
the poet must never forget that his final quest
is beauty.

Although, with regard to the question as to
what is and what is not a subject debarred by
its inherent repulsiveness from poetical treatment, there can be no formulated rule, yet for
a poet to approach repulsive subjects is in the
last degree dangerous. Almost everything, however, depends upon the treatment and the
temper of the poet. If these be sufficiently
heroic to conquer the conditions of the repulsive
surroundings, the work even of a surgeon's
scalpel in the gruesome cockpit of a man-of-war
may become poetic and beautiful ; and if the
man under the surgeon's hands be Horatio
Nelson, whispering to his brother hero bending
over him, " Kiss me, Hardy," the entire poetic
picture may be sublime.

Of Dante's work, this faculty of seizing upon
the salient and representative facts of nature
and transfiguring them in the fiery crucible of
his unequalled imagination is the prominent
characteristic. What he sees he flashes upon
the actual retina of him who listens to his song,
and this he often does by means of details
which are essentially prose details selected by

the poet's eye. The Dantesque realism is simply an attempt of a marvellously intense imagination to get as close as possible to the physiognomy of nature and of human nature. And the same poetic eye for selecting from the materials of prose is seen when we come to consider such secondary, but still great luminaries as Villon and Burns. Without a very large endowment of this high quality where would be the most characteristic lyrics of either of these poets ? And Crabbe's realism is quite as true as theirs, though he lacked that sense of beauty and that intensity of vision which alone brings the supreme power of selection belonging to the greatest artists.

To write melodious verses like the " Adonais " of Shelley, or gorgeously coloured verses like Keats's " Endymion," is no doubt, to do a beautiful and a worthy work, for in the poetic heaven there are many mansions. Indeed, the reader who cannot dally with and enjoy the lovely rhapsody of the " Ode to the West Wind," and even the golden toy " Sleep and Poetry," may almost be said to lack the poetic sense. Nay, we might go further, and say that it is in the power of producing such poetic bubbles as Coleridge's " Kubla Khan," that the magic gift of the poet, as distinguished from the prose-man, is sometimes most clearly seen. For if we were asked to bring forward the most complete example of pure poetry unmixed with any of these qualities which poetry shares in common with prose—unmixed, for instance, with passion or thought—we should certainly instance

" Kubla Khan," where there is nothing but
that blending of colour and music with imaginative feeling which forms the pabulum of the
poetic dream when the vision has plunged right
away into the deepest recesses of dreamland.
To show the power of writing such a fantasia
as Coleridge's is to show an endowment more
truly poetic (in the narrowest sense) than the
power to write a poem of immeasurably nobler
temper—such a poem, for instance as " Laodamia "—for there is no smallest portion of
" Kubla Khan " that could have been touched
by the fingers of prose.

Having admitted so much as this, why do we
affirm of Spenser, Shelley, Coleridge, and Keats
that between such work as theirs and the work
of the others we have named, from Homer down
to Villon and Burns, the difference is one of
kind, and that the latter kind of poetry has in
it a deeper vitality than the former ? The
answer to this question is easy enough. Now
to do this an amount of realism is required
such as can only be compassed by a close study
of the external world.

Therefore, although in admiration of Shelley
and Keats we yield to none, it is because we do
not find, save in a very few of their noblest
works, that loving eye for the physiognomy of
life—whether it be the life of nature or the life
of man—which we find in even the smallest of
the poets we have contrasted with them.

Perhaps the reason why so few poets of the
most intensely poetical kind have been able to
import realism into poetry is that the command

over the mere poetic vehicle which we see in poets like Shelley and Keats is so prodigious, and involves such an entire devotion to the study of poetry as a fine art, that but little force is left for the study of nature and man—that study, in short, which and which alone, can result in the poetic realism of those great masters who combine all the powers of the two varieties of poets.

Realism, then, is not only a legitimate, it is an essential quest of the poet until he has passed into that high mood when, in his passion of prophecy, he can see nothing between his tripod and the heaven of which he sings. Yet there is, beyond any question, a limit to the extent to which the poet may invade the domain of the prose writer and steal from the garden of prose the proper nutriment for the poet's fairy land.

It cannot be said that " Isabella " shows Keats to have had any ear for the ottava rima as a vehicle of serious poetry. As to what he would have done with it in mock-heroic, his treatment of the Spenserian stanza in " The Cap and Bells " was not so successful as to make critics wish that he had given them a cockney " Don Juan."

The crown of worldly verse is seen in the mock heroic and the greatest master of mock heroic in all literature is Byron.

It was after the first two cantos of " Childe Harold " that Byron awoke and found himself famous. It is difficult to understand why, for not even the after cantos were good enough to place him alongside the immortal poets of the

world.　It is his worldly verse—it is in such
great masterpieces as " The Vision of Judgment" and " Don Juan "—that his place is
immortal.　He first found his true wings in
" Beppo," a marvel of wit and worldly wisdom.
Then came " The Vision of Judgment," where
on the wings of worldly verse he soars away
almost into that region of the sublime which he
sought in " Childe Harold," " Manfred," " Cain,"
&c., and never reached.　Then came " Don
Juan," by far the greatest piece of worldly verse
in any language.　All these are, of course,
written in ottava rima, the only English stanza
that Byron ever mastered.　Although this
measure has been successfully used for serious
poetry, as in Tasso's " La Gerusalemme
Liberata," in Fairfax's translation of it, and
with less success in Keats's " Isabella," the
proper moving spirit of the ottava rima is
jauntiness.　The ottava rima was suggested to
Byron, not apparently by the Italian poets, but
by Frere in " Whistlecraft," where it is used
with admirable ease and effect.　From this
moment Byron's success as a poet was assured.
It may be said that it is only in ottava rima,
the proper medium for worldly poetry that
Byron is likely to take his place among the
immortals.

The present writer has on a former occasion
enlarged upon the inherent suggestion of jauntiness in ottava rima.　He has said that it is
just as much an impertinence there as it is in
real life, unless the poet makes jauntiness a
good weight-carrier.　The same horse whose

prancings in his box, unburdened by saddle or
rider, seem so clumsy and ridiculous, looks a
very different creature when he caracols with
ten stone upon his back. In seeing a man
jauntily touch the strings of a guitar there is
nothing exhilarating at all. But when one of
those Japanese acrobats whose incredible feats
strike the spectator with awe, displays his
jauntiness, jauntily touches the strings of his
guitar as he balances on his shoulder a bamboo
which is curved almost to a semi-circle by the
weight of another acrobat twisting and twirling
like a monkey at the top, but twisting and
twirling in the perfectly contented knowledge
that absolute safety to his own neck lies in the
genius of the man below, then the jauntiness
of such guitar-playing as that adds to the
wonder of the performance.

Now we do not mean to say that a recognition
of difficulty overcome, though undoubtedly an
element of the pleasure we derive from poetry,
is the most important element, even in mock-
heroic poetry, but assuredly it is at the bottom
of all the pleasure we derive from the jaunting,
as properly expressed by the fifth and sixth
lines of ottava rima.

For, to show that the poet can do playfully
all that the heroic does seriously is the work
of the serio-comic ottava rima—Italian or
English. The reader should feel that here is
one who could scale Parnassus with the best of
them, if he would, but that in the riot of his
power he lingers to disport himself on its lower
slopes. But then it is essential to have the

power before you can play with it. Here is the
difficulty ; and now it is that we come to the
secret why the serio-comic ottava rima is not
to be achieved by the mere word-kneader,
knead he never so wisely. It is not born of
artifice at all. It is the natural expression of a
mood—a mood unknown to schoolboys, and to
poets who are as school-boys bounded in their
playground lives—the mood of the full-blooded
man who has lived—who, if in his time he has
laughed more than most other men, has very
likely wept more than most ; who, if he has
enjoyed more than most other men, has very
likely suffered more than most, and who is
alive even yet to the beauty and the pathos
of human life.

Byron has had many imitators, and as many
failures. But no one has written a single stanza
in ottava rima that could be mistaken for one
of his stanzas. In the case of Byron's ottava
rima all that the imitator can catch is the
jauntiness. Perhaps it was his feeling this that
made Browning when writing " The Two Poets
of Croisic " in ottava rima adopt the variation
of the stanza.

It is difficult to say—judging from this poem
—what Browning could, and what he could not,
do with the ottava rima ; for here he has evidently been working in accordance with some
theory.

One of the requisites of English ottava rima
used for humorous purposes is to give it
Italian lightness every now and then by the
use of double rhymes, and sometimes even of

triple rhymes. Now Browning is a greater master of difficult rhyming than Byron himself—the greatest indeed since Butler—but in " The Two Poets of Croisic " there is not one double or triple rhyme. Why is this ? Is it because the moment double and triple rhymes are used in English ottava rima the jaunty effect which they give makes the poem seem an echo of " Don Juan," " Beppo," " Whistlecraft " ? If so, it is of course no wonder that Browning—the most truly original poet of his time—should be shy of running such a risk. But, on the other hand, jauntiness seems essential to English ottava rima used for comic narrative.

The fifth and sixth lines, in which the lines of the quatrains are repeated, are imported expressly to " turn into play " what has been said seriously before, and the epigrammatic summing up comes in the couplet. If the charm of the poem consists, as in "The Two Poets of Croisic," in strings of brilliant epigrams merely, there was no need to use the ottava rima ; the " Venus and Adonis " stanza would have done the work better.

III

THE POSITION OF POETRY IN RELATION TO THE OTHER ARTS

HAVING now considered the function of worldly and unworldly verse, we are prepared to ask the question of the relation of poetry to the other arts. This was never so uncertain and anomalous as at the present moment. On the one hand there is a class of critics who, judging from their perpetual comparison of poems to pictures, claim her as a sort of handmaid of painting and sculpture. On the other hand the disciples of Wagner, while professing to do homage to poetry, claim her as the handmaid of music. To find her proper place is therefore the most important task the critic can undertake at this time, though it is one far beyond the scope of a work so brief as this. With regard to the relations of poetry to painting and sculpture, however, it seems necessary to glance for a moment at the saying of Simonides, as recorded by Plutarch, that poetry is a speaking picture, and that painting is a mute poetry. It appears to have had upon modern criticism as much influence since the publication of Lessing's Laocoon as it had before. Perhaps it is in some measure answerable for the modern vice of excessive word-painting. Beyond this one saying, there is little or nothing in Greek literature to show that the Greeks recognised between poetry and the plastic and pictorial arts an affinity closer than that which exists between poetry and music and dancing. Understanding artistic methods more profoundly than the moderns, and far too profoundly to suppose that there is any special and peculiar affinity between an art whose medium of expression is marble and an art whose medium of expression is a growth of oral symbols, the Greeks seem to have studied poetry not so much in its relation to painting and sculpture as in its relation to music and dancing. It is matter of familiar knowledge, for instance, that at the Dionysian festival it was to the poet as " teacher of the chorus " (χοροδιδάσκαλος) that the prize was awarded, even though the " teacher of the chorus " were Æschylus himself or Sophocles. And this recognition of the relation of poetry to music is perhaps one of the many causes of the superiority of Greek to all other poetry in adapting artistic means to artistic ends.

In Greek poetry, even in Homer's description of the shield of Achilles, even in the famous description by Sophocles of his native woods in the Œdipus Coloneus, such word-painting as occurs seems, if not inevitable and unconscious, so alive with imaginative feeling as to become part and parcel of the dramatic or lyric movement itself. And whenever description is so introduced the reader of Greek poetry need not be told that the scenery itself rises before the listener's imagination with a clearness of outline and a vigour of colour such as no amount of detailed word-painting in the modern fashion can achieve. The picture even in the glorious verses at the end of the eighth book of the Iliad rises before our eyes—seems actually to act upon our bodily senses—simply because the poet's eagerness to use the picture for merely illustrating the solemnity and importance of his story lends to the picture that very authenticity which the work of the modern word-painter lacks.

That the true place of poetry lies between music on the one hand and prose, or loosened speech, on the other, was, we say, taken for granted by the one people in whom the artistic instinct was fully developed.

No doubt they used the word music in a very wide sense, in a sense that might include several arts. But it is a suggestive fact that, in the Greek language, long before poetic art was called " making," it was called " singing." The poet was not ποιητής but ἀοιδός. And as regards the Romans it is curious to see how every now and then the old idea that poetry is singing rather than making will disclose itself. It will be remembered, for instance, how Terence, in the prologue of Phormio, alludes to poets as musicians. That the ancients were right in this we should be able to show did our scheme permit an historical treatment of poetry, we should be able to show that music and the lyrical function of the poet began together, but that here, as in other things, the progress of art from the implicit to the explicit has separated the two.

Every art has its special function, has a certain work which it can do better than any one of its sister arts. Hence its right of existence. For instance, before the " sea of emotion " within the soul has become " curdled

into thoughts," it can be expressed in inarticulate tone. Hence, among the fine arts,
music is specially adapted for rendering it.
It was perhaps a perception of this fact which
made the Syrian Gnostics define life to be
" moving music." When this sea of emotion
has " curdled into thoughts," articulate language rhythmically arranged—words steeped
in music and colour, but at the same time
embodying ideas—can do what no mere word-
less music is able to achieve in giving it expression, just as unrhythmical language, language mortised in a foundation of logic that
is to say prose, can best express these ideas as
soon as they have cooled and settled and
cleared themselves of emotion altogether.

Yet every art can in some degree invade the
domain of her sisters, and the nearer these
sisters stand to each other the more easily and
completely can this invasion be accomplished.
Prose, for instance, can sometimes, as in the
case of Plato, do some of the work of poetry
(however imperfectly, and however trammelled
by heavy conditions) ; and sometimes poetry,
as in Pindar's odes and the waves of the Greek
chorus, can do, though in the same imperfect
way the work of music. The poems of Sappho,

however, are perhaps the best case in point.
Here the poet's passion is expressed so completely by the mere sound of her verses that a
good recitation of them to a person ignorant
of Greek would convey something of that passion
to the listener ; and similar examples almost as
felicitous might be culled from Homer, from
Æschylus, and from Sophocles. Nor is this
power confined to the Greek poets. The
students of Virgil have often and with justice
commented on such lines as Æn v. 481 (where
the sudden sinking of a stricken ox is rendered
by means of rhythm), and such lines as Georg.
ii. 441, where, by means of verbal sounds, the
gusts of wind about a tree are rendered as
completely as though the voice were that of
the wind itself.

In the case of Sappho the effect is produced
by the intensity of her passion, in the case of
Homer by the intensity of the dramatic vision,
in the case of Virgil by a supreme poetic art.
But it can also be produced by the mere ingenuity of the artist, as in Edgar Poe's " Ulalume." The poet's object in that remarkable
tour de force was to express dull and hopeless
gloom in the same way that the mere musician
would have expressed it—that is to say, by

monotonous reiterations, by hollow and dreadful reverberations of gloomy sounds—though
as an artist whose vehicle was articulate speech
he was obliged to add gloomy ideas, in order
to give to his work the intellectual coherence
necessary for its existence as a poem. He
evidently set out to do this, and he did it, and
" Ulalume " properly intoned would produce
something like the same effect upon a listener
knowing no word of English that it produces
upon us.

Comparing poetry with music, there is more
of music's peculiar and special and essential
witchery in the meaningless strains struck out
by the wind from the "thunderharp of pines,"
or from an Æolian harp hung in a window than
in any of the greatest compositions of Beethoven
or Wagner. But then there is the associative
effect of music to be taken into account—
those simple and deathless airs that play upon
every chord of the human soul and every nerve
of the human body—airs such as the " Mar-
seillaise" on the one hand, and "Home Sweet
Home " on the other.

And this is because, although poetry is one
of the fine arts, it is also much more than one
of the fine arts. It is the final expression of the
whole genial nature of man, and aspires to read
all the symbols of the universe in which man
is placed.

As to what languages are the most musical,

that can never be decided. The speakers of
each language will decide for themselves.

It is, however, pathetic to think that the
inherent beauty of any language has but little
to do with its chance of survival in the great
linguistic struggle for life. Here, indeed, as
in every other part of nature's great scheme of
evolution, no heed is given to beauty. When
she does achieve beauty it seems to be by
accident. What functions are useful ? What
functions are useless ? These only are the
questions answered by the history of nations
and their languages as by the history of nature.
Who would have supposed that human speech
starting from the gorilla roar (which Du Chaillu
alone among human beings could dare to
render), and reaching at length that divine
tongue in which Sappho sang, should get no
higher ? Those who have listened to the
nightingales at Fiesole must have often asked
themselves whether the birds alone are to
monopolize the perfection of speech, which is,
of course, to talk in music—whether in this
regard man is to stay where he is, half-way
between unmusical beasts and the musical
birds.

If " evolution " and " progress " were synonymous terms, would not human speech have gone
on from Greek, (softening, indeed, in some degree
eliminating, those sibilants which vexed the
poetic ear of Pindar and the critical soul of
Dionysius of Halicarnassus), until it became
as soft and full of liquids as Italian, but without losing any of the strength and grandeur and

pathos of the tongue of Sophocles ? Would it not have gone on until the perfect human tongue was evolved—a tongue so musical that the moment the speaker passed into passionate utterance he would be obliged to sing instead of speak his emotions ?

On the other hand, music can trench very far upon the domain of articulate speech, as we perceive in the wonderful instrumentation of Wagner. Yet, while it can be shown that the place of poetry is scarcely so close to sculpture and painting as to music on the one side and loosened speech on the other, the affinity of poetry to music must not be exaggerated. We must be cautious how we follow the canons of Wagner and the more enthusiastic of his disciples, who almost seem to think that inarticulate tone can not only suggest ideas, but express them—can give voice to the *Verstand*, in short, as well as to the *Vernunft* of man. Even the Greeks drew a fundamental distinction between melic poetry (poetry written to be sung) and poetry that was written to be recited. It is a pity that, while modern critics of poetry have understood, or at least have given attention to painting and sculpture, so few have possessed any knowledge of music—a fact which makes Dante's treatise *De Vulgari Eloquio* so important. Dante was a musician, and seems to have had a considerable knowledge of the relations between musical and metrical laws. But he did not, we think, assume that these laws are identical.

If it is indeed possible to establish the identity of musical and metrical laws, it can only be done by a purely scientific investigation ; it can only be done by a most searching inquiry into the subtle relations that we know must exist throughout the universe between all the laws of undulation. And it is curious to remember that some of the greatest masters of verbal melody have had no knowledge of music, while some have not even shown any love of it.

All Greek boys were taught music, but whether Pindar's unusual musical skill was born of natural instinct and inevitable passion, or came from the accidental circumstance that his father was, as he has been alleged, a musician, and that he was as a boy elaborately taught musical science by Lasus of Hermione, we have no means of knowing. Nor can we now learn how much of Milton's musical knowledge resulted from a like exceptional " environment," or from the fact that his father was a musician. But when we find that Shelley seems to have

been without the real passion for music, that
Rossetti disliked it, that Swinburne was indifferent to it, and that Coleridge's apprehension
of musical effects was of the ordinary nebulous
kind, we must hesitate before accepting the
theory of Wagner.

The question cannot be pursued here, but if
it should on inquiry be found that, although
poetry is more closely related to music than to
any of the other arts, yet the power over verbal
melody at its very highest is so all-sufficing to
its possessor, as in the case of Shelley and
Coleridge that absolute music becomes a super-
fluity, this would be another illustration of
that intense egoism and concentration of force
—the impulse of all high artistic energy—which
is required in order to achieve the rarest miracles
of art.

It could easily be proved that the structural
difference between poetry and prose is fundamental. Among the many delights which we
get from the mere form of what is technically
called Poetry, the chief, perhaps, is expectation
and the fulfilment of expectation. This is
very obvious in rhymed verse, having familiarized ourselves with the arrangement of the
poet's rhymes, we take pleasure in expecting
a recurrence of these rhymes according to this
arrangement. In blank verse the law of ex-

pectation is less apparent. Yet it is none the less operative. Having familiarized ourselves with the poet's rhythm, having found that iambic foot succeeds iambic foot, and that whenever the iambic waves have begun to grow monotonous, variations occur—trochaic, ana-pæstic, dactylic—according to the law which governs the ear of this individual poet ; we, half consciously, expect at certain intervals these variations, and are delighted when our expectations are fulfilled. And our delight is augmented if also our expectations with regard to cæsuric effects are realised in the same pro-portions. Having, for instance, learned, half unconsciously, that the poet has an ear for a particular kind of pause, that he delights, let us say, to throw his pause after the third foot of the sequence,—we expect that, whatever may be the arrangement of the early pauses with regard to the initial foot of any sequence,—there must be, not far ahead, that climacteric third-foot pause up to which all the other pauses have been tending, and upon which the ear and the soul of the reader shall be allowed to rest to take breath for future flights. And when this ex-pectation of cæsuric effects is thus gratified, or gratified in a more subtle way, by an arrange-ment of earlier semi-pauses, which obviates the necessity of the too frequent recurrence of this final third-foot pause, the full pleasure of poetic effects is the result. In other words, a large proportion of the pleasure we derive from poetry is in the *recognition* of law. The more obvious and formulated is the law,—nay, the more arbitrary and Draconian—the more pleasure it gives to the uncultivated ear. This is why uneducated people may delight in rhyme, and yet have no ear at all for blank verse ; this is why the savage, who has not even an ear for rhyme, takes pleasure in such unmistakable rhythm as that of his tom-tom. But, as the ear becomes more cultivated, it demands that these indications of law should be more and more subtle, till at last recognised law itself may become a tyranny and a burden. He who will read Shakespeare's plays chronologically, as far as that is practicable from " Love's Labour's Lost " to the " Tempest," will have no difficulty in seeing precisely what we mean. In literature, as in social life, the progress is from lawless freedom, through tyranny, to freedom that is lawful.

There are indications already that this axiom is likely to be acted upon by the poets of the twentieth century, but they must mind that they do not carry it too far ; lawless freedom may become anarchy.

With regard to the relation of poetry to prose, Coleridge once asserted in conversation that the real antithesis of poetry was not prose but science. And if he was right the difference in kind lies, not between the poet and the prose writer, but between the literary artist (the man whose instinct is to manipulate language) and the man of facts and of action whose instinct impels him to act, or, if not to act, to inquire,

One thing is at least certain, that prose, however fervid and emotional it may become, must
always be directed, or seem to be directed by
the reins of logic. Or, to vary the metaphor,
like a captive balloon it can never really leave
the earth.

Indeed, with the literature of knowledge as
opposed to the literature of power poetry has
nothing to do. Facts have no place in poetry
until they are brought into relation with the
human soul. But a mere catalogue of ships
may become poetical if it tends to show the
strength and pride and glory of the warriors
who invested Troy ; a detailed description of
the designs upon a shield, however beautiful
and poetical in itself, becomes still more so if it
tends to show the skill of the divine artificer
and the invincible splendour of a hero like
Achilles. But mere dry exactitude of imitation
is not for poetry, but for "loosened speech,"
as the Greeks called prose. Hence, most of the
so-called poetry of Hesiod is not poetry at all.
The Muses who spoke to him about "truth"
on Mount Helicon made the common mistake
of confounding fact with truth.

And here we touch upon a very important
matter. The reason why in prose speech is

loosened is that, untrammelled by the laws of
metre, language is able with more exactitude
to imitate nature, though of course speech, even
when " loosened " cannot, when actual sensible
objects are to be depicted, compete in any real
degree with the plastic arts in accuracy of
imitation, for the simple reason that its media
are not colours nor solids, but symbols—
arbitrary symbols which can be made to in-
dicate, but never to reproduce colours and
solids. Accuracy of imitation is the first requisite of prose. But the moment language has
to be governed by the laws of metre—the
moment the conflict begins between the claims
of verbal music and the claims of colour and
form—then prosaic accuracy has to yield,
sharpness of outline, mere fidelity of imitation,
such as is within the compass of prose, have
in some degree to be sacrificed. But, just as
with regard to the relations between poetry and
music the greatest master is he who borrows
the most that can be borrowed from music,
and loses the least that can be lost from metre,
so with regard to the relations between poetry
and prose the greatest master is he who borrows
the most that can be borrowed from prose and
loses the least that can be lost from verse. No

doubt this is what every poet tries to do by instinct ; but some sacrifice on either side there must be, and, with regard to poetry and prose, modern poets at least might be divided into those who make picturesqueness yield to verbal melody, and those who make verbal melody yield to picturesqueness.

With one class of poets, fine as is perhaps the melody, it is made subservient to outline or to colour ; with the other class colour and outline both yield to metre. The chief aim of the first-class is to paint a picture ; the chief aim of the second is to sing a song. Weber, in driving through a beautiful country could only enjoy its beauty by translating it into music. The same may be said of some poets with regard to verbal melody. The supreme artist, however, is he whose pictorial and musical power are so interfused that each seems born of the other, as is the case with Sappho, Homer, Æschylus, Sophocles, and indeed most of the Greek poets.

Among our own poets (leaving the two supreme masters undiscussed) Keats and Coleridge have certainly done this. The colour seems born of the music, and the music born of the colour. In French poetry the same triumph has been achieved in Victor Hugo's magnificent poem " En Marchant la Nuit dans un Bois," which, as a rendering through verbal music of the witchery of nature, stands alone in the poetry of France. For there the poet conquers that crowning difficulty we have been alluding to, the difficulty of stealing from prose as much distinctness of colour and clearness of outline as can be imported into verse with as little sacrifice as possible of melody.

But to return to the general relations of poetry to prose. If poetry can in some degree invade the domain of prose, so on the other hand prose can at times invade the domain of poetry, and no doubt the prose of Plato—what is called poetical prose—is a legitimate form of art. Poetry, the earliest form of literature, is also the final and ideal form of all pure literature ; and when Landor insists that poetry and poetical prose are antagonistic, we must re-member that Landor's judgments are mostly based on feeling, and that his hatred of Plato would be quite sufficient basis with him for an entire system of criticism upon poetical prose. As with Carlyle, there seems to have been a time in his life when Plato (who of course is the great figure standing between the two arts of metre and loosened speech) had serious thoughts of becoming a poet.   And perhaps like Carlyle, having the good sense to see his true function, he himself desisted from writing, and strictly forbade other men to write in verse.

If we consider this, and if we consider that certain of the great English masters of poetic prose of the seventeenth century were apparently as incapable of writing in metre as their followers Richter and Carlyle, we shall hardly escape the conclusion on the one hand that the faculty of writing poetry is quite another faculty than that of producing work in the kindred art of prose.

If we confess—as we are going to confess—that poetry, howsoever powerful, sometimes fails to give us the pleasure we ask from a poet, we know exactly the kind of answer that will be in store for us. It will be said " The Question as to what subjects are, and what subjects are not fit for poetic treatment is one which will never be settled, for in these matters a great deal must depend upon temperament."

Without again going over the old ground of the quaint American heresy which seems to affirm that the great masters of metrical music, from Homer to Tennyson and Swinburne, have been blowing through penny trumpets " feudal ideas " (whatever " feudal ideas " may be), and that the more unmetrical the lines the more free do they become from the penny trumpet and the " feudal ideas," we may say this in reference to all metrical structures, whether quantitative or accentual, whether rhymed or unrhymed—that where the cæsura at the end of a verse, whether a rhyme cæsura or a quantitative cæsura, is so strong that the ear expects a certain kind of responsive emphasis in the subsequent verse or verses, the expectation must be gratified, or there is artistic failure.   This is why, when in modern versification quantity came to be supplanted by accent, so many languages adopted alliteration, or assonance, or rhyme.   And as regards English poetry, the moment that rhyme emphasis supplanted the alliterative emphasis which preceded it, rhymeless verses became impossible, save in the measure we call " fluent blank verse."

As for such so-called rhythmical movements as we get in " The Lily and the Bee," " Proverbial Philosophy," "Leaves of Grass," etc., these have, apparently, nothing whatever to do with what Chaucer in the " House of Fame " calls cadence—if we may judge from the " Tale of Milibœus."

What Chaucer meant by " cadence " was evidently a kind of measured prose with no pretensions to metrical structure, though, being measured, it was enabled to escape at will that severe logical sequence demanded in all purely prose compositions.   But in each of the modern cases instanced above the writer endeavours to escape the conditions of both prose and verse— endeavours to escape, that is to say, the logical march of the one and the metric scheme of the other. They are, indeed, caricatures of Bible rhythm—that divine movement compared with which even the music of Shakespeare and Milton seems almost jejune—the movement which, as Selden has said, was the happy result of the translators endeavouring to give in English the bars of the sense-rhythm of the original. " The Bible," says he, " is rather translated into English words than into English phrase. The Hebraisms are kept, and the phrase of that language is kept."

To discuss the metrical movements of the most famous innovator in this line, Walt. Whitman, has become positively painful, especially to those who sympathise with the liberal and generous views these innovations embody ; but it would be uncandid to shrink from saying that the endeavour to imitate this movement of our sublime English Bible in poems where the jargon of the slums is mixed up with Bible phraseology and bad Spanish and worse French is a sacrilege which every lover of the Bible finds it hard to condone. Some rhymeless verses, however, are not caricatures of this kind : some are governed by a stanzaic law which is something like that governing the " Kalevala " rhythm of Longfellow's rhymeless verses. Its effect is to enfeeble the substance, however strong. A trochee at the end of even a long English verse is so strong that the ear demands a rhyme response. But in short lines this demand becomes quite inexorable.

In judging of any young and inexperienced adventurer on Parnassus the first thing after enquiring into his merits is to inquire whether such defects as he displays come from mere inexperience, or from the fact that his metric art is the art of arithmetic—his rhythmic rule the cobbler's " rule of thumb." And perhaps there is no more infallible sign of the poetaster who rhymes not because a natural impulse forces him to rhyme, but because other people rhyme, than his horror of " fluent rhyming " and his love of " hard rhyming " on all occasions. Such a poet goes to his work in exactly the same spirit that the mathematician goes to his lines and angles. He has sufficient apprehension of the sounds of his mother tongue to perceive that while " Jove " is a hard rhyme to " love," " move," and "grove " are not ; and that while " dome " is a hard rhyme to " home," " come " is not. Even he can perceive this ; and at once he feels that he has made a discovery. He takes a solemn oath that nothing on earth shall induce him to use the makeshift rhymes of Shakespeare and the rest ; that nothing on earth shall ever induce him to write such a stanza as :—

> Strong son of God, immortal love,
>   Whom we, that have not seen thy face,
>   By faith, and faith alone, embrace,
> Believing where we cannot prove—

when it is so easy to rhyme " love " with " above," or " glove," that nothing in the world shall ever induce him to write such a stanza as :—

Never, though my mortal summers through such
   length of years shall come,
As the many-wintered crow that leads the clanging
   rookery home—

when it is so easy to rhyme " come " with
" drum " or " rule of thumb." " All the English poets," he says, " have used such rhymes
under compulsion of the exigencies of form—
perish the exigencies of form ! "

The young versifier who is also a poet, howsoever ignorant he may be of metrical science,
feels that the harmonies of our great poets are
not used for makeshift purposes ; that, on the
contrary, this fluent rhyming gives him, the
young poet, that artistic satisfaction of a sense
of cadence which is of all intellectual delights
the greatest. And as he grows older and bolder,
and comes to know his business more thoroughly,
the more freely does he rhyme " love " with
" move " and " grove," " home " with " come,"
and even " ever " with " river." He per-
ceives that, owing to the blending of consonantal with vowel power, such fluent rhymes
as these are not only as good as hard
rhymes, but in many cases very much better,
for in long sequences hard rhyming, though
grateful at first, may begin to pall. The theory
of rhyming cannot be entered upon here ; but
perhaps what Bacon says in reference to another
matter is applicable to fluent rhyming as a
change from hard rhyming. " The sliding,"
says he, " in the close or cadence hath an agree-
ment with the figure in rhetorick which they call
præter expectatum, for there is a pleasure in

being deceived." Indeed, rhymes like " come " and " home " are sufficiently near to hard rhymes to gratify the expectation of the ear, and yet they give that soupçon of variety and surprise which true poets and true readers of poetry love.

So much for poetry's mere place among the other arts.

IV

COMPARATIVE VALUE IN EXPRESSIONAL POWER

THERE is one great point of superiority that musical art exhibits over metrical art. This consists, not in the capacity for melody, but in the capacity for harmony in the musician's sense. The finest music of Æschylus, of Pindar, of Shakespeare, of Milton, is after all only a succession of melodious notes, and, in endeavouring to catch the harmonic intent of strophe, antistrophe and epode in the Greek chorus, and in the true ode (that of Pindar), we can only succeed by pressing memory into our service. We have to recall by memory the waves that have gone before, and then to imagine their harmonic power in relation to the waves at present occupying the ear. Counterpoint, therefore, is not to be achieved by the metricist, even though he be Pindar himself; but in music this perfect ideal harmony was foreshadowed perhaps in the earliest writing.

We know at least that as early as the twelfth century counterpoint began to show a vigorous life, and the study of it is now a familiar branch of musical science.

Now, inasmuch as " Nature's own hymn " is and must be the harmonic blending of apparently independent and apparently discordant notes, among the arts whose appeal is through the ear that which can achieve counterpoint must perhaps rank as a pure art above one which cannot achieve it. We are, of course, speaking here of metre only. We have not space to inquire whether the counterpoint of absolute poetry is the harmony underlying apparently discordant emotions—the emotion produced by a word being more persistent than the emotion produced by an inarticulate sound.

But if poetry falls behind music in rhythmic scope it is capable of rendering emotion after emotion has become disintegrated into thoughts, and here, as we have seen, it enters into direct competition with the art of prose. It can use the emphasis of sound, not for its own sake merely, but to strengthen the emphasis of sense and can thus give a fuller and more adequate expression to the soul of man than music at its highest can give. With regard to prose, no doubt such writing as Plato's description of the chariot of the soul, his description of the island of Atlantis, or of Er's visit to the place of departed souls, comes but a short way behind poetry in imaginative and even in rhythmic appeal. It is impossible, however, here to do more than touch upon the subject of the rhythm of prose in its relation to the rhythm of poetry ; for in this matter the genius of each individual language has to be taken into account.

Perhaps it may be said that deeper than all the rhythms of art is that rhythm which art would fain catch, the rhythm of nature ; for the rhythm of nature is the rhythm of life itself. This rhythm can be caught by prose as well as by poetry, such prose, for instance, as that of the English Bible. Certainly the rhythm of verse at its highest, such, for instance, as that of Shakespeare's greatest writings, is nothing more and nothing less than the metre of that energy of the spirit which surges within the bosom of him who speaks, whether he speak in verse or in impassioned prose. Being rhythm, it is of course governed by law, but it is a law which transcends in subtlety the conscious art of the metricist, and is only caught by the poet in his most inspired moods, a law, which, being part of nature's own sanctions, can of course never be formulated but only expressed, as it is expressed in the melody of the bird, in the inscrutable harmony of the entire bird chorus of a thicket, in the whisper of the leaves of the tree, and in the song or wail of wind and sea.

Now is not this rhythm of nature represented by that " sense rhythm " which prose can catch as well as poetry, that sense rhythm whose finest expressions are to be found in the Bible, Hebrew and English, and in the Biblical movements of the English Prayer Book, and in the dramatic prose of Shakespeare at its best ? Whether it is caught by prose or by verse, one of the virtues of the rhythm of nature is that it is translatable. Hamlet's peroration about man and Raleigh's apostrophe to death are as translatable into other languages as are the Hebrew psalms, or as is Manu's magnificent passage about the singleness of man :—

" Single is each man born into the world ; single he dies ; single he receives the reward of his good deeds, and single the punishment of his evil deeds. When he dies his body lies like a fallen tree upon the earth, but his virtue accompanies his soul. Wherefore let man harvest and garner virtue, so that he may have an inseparable companion in traversing that gloom which is so hard to be traversed."

Here the "rhythm," being the inevitable movement of emotion and "sense," can be caught and translated by every literature under the sun. While, however, the great goal before the poet is to compel the listener to expect his cæsuric effects, the great goal before the writer of poetic prose is in the very opposite direction ; it is to make use of the concrete figures and impassioned diction of the poet, but at the same time to avoid the recognized and expected metrical bars upon which the poet depends. The moment the prose poet passes from the rhythm of prose to the ryhthm of metre the apparent sincerity of his writing is destroyed.

As compared with sculpture and painting the great infirmity of poetry, as an "imitation." of nature, is of course that the medium is always and of necessity words—even when no words could, in the dramatic situation, have been spoken. It is not only Homer who is obliged sometimes to forget that passion when at white heat is never voluble, is scarcely even articulate, the dramatists also are obliged to forget that in love and in hate, at their tensest, words seem weak and foolish when compared with the silent and satisfying triumph and glory of deeds, such as the plastic arts can render. This becomes manifest enough when we compare the Niobe group or the Laocoon group, or the great dramatic paintings of the modern world, with even the finest efforts of dramatic poetry, such as the speech of Andromache to Hector, or the speech of Priam to Achilles, nay such as even the cries of Cassandra in the Agamemnon, or the wailings of Lear over the dead Cordelia.

Even when writing the words uttered by Œdipus as the terrible truth breaks in upon his soul, Sophocles must have felt that, in the holiest chambers of sorrow, and in the highest agonies of suffering reigns that awful silence which not poetry, but painting sometimes, and sculpture always, can render. What human sounds could render the agony of Niobe, or the agony of Laocoon, as we see them in the sculptor's rendering ? Not articulate speech at all ; not words, but wails.

It is the same with hate ; it is the same with love. We are not speaking merely of the unpacking of the heart in which the angry warriors of the Iliad indulge. Even such subtle writing as that of Æschylus and Sophocles falls below the work of the painter. Hate, though voluble perhaps, as Clytæmnestra's when hate is at that red-heat glow which the poet can render, changes in a moment whenever that redness has been fanned to hatred's own last complexion —whiteness as of iron at the melting-point— when the heart has grown far too big to be " unpacked " at all, and even the bitter epigrams of hate's own rhetoric, though brief as the terrier's snap before he fleshes his teeth, or as the short snarl of the tigress as she springs before her cubs in danger, are all too slow and sluggish for a soul to which language at its tensest has become idle play. But this is just what cannot be rendered by an art whose medium consists solely of words.

It is in giving voice, not to emotion at its tensest, but to the vibrations of emotion, it is in expressing the countless shifting movements of the soul from passion to passion, that poetry shows in spite of all her infirmities her superiority to the plastic arts. Hamlet and the Agamemnon, the Iliad, and the Œdipus Tyrannus, are adequate to the entire breadth and depth of man's soul.

V

VARIETIES OF POETIC ART

WE have now reached our last general inquiry—What varieties of poetic art are the outcome of the two kinds of poetic impulse, dramatic imagination and lyric or egoistic imagination ? It would, of course, be impossible here to examine fully the subject of poetic imagination. For in order to do so we should have to enter upon the vast question of the effect of artistic environment upon the development of man's poetic imagination ; we should have to inquire how the instinctive methods of each poet, and of each group of poets have been modified and often governed by the methods characteristic of their own time and country. We should have to inquire, for instance, how far such landscape as that of Sophocles in the Œdipus Coloneus and such landscape as that of Wordsworth, depends upon difference of individual temperament, and how far upon difference of artistic environment. That, in any thorough and exhaustive discussion of poetic imagination, the question of artistic environment must be taken into account, the case of the Iliad is alone sufficient to show. Ages before Phrynichus, ages before an acted drama was dreamed of, a dramatic poet of the first order arose, and, though he was obliged to express his splendid dramatic imagination through epic forms, he expressed it almost as fully as if he had inherited the method and the stage of Sophocles. And if Homer never lived at all, then an entire group of dramatic poets arose in remote times, whose method was epic instead of dramatic simply because there was then no stage.

This, contrasted with the fact that in a single half-century the tragic art of Greece arose with Æschylus, culminated with Sophocles, and decayed with Euripides, and contrasted also with the fact that in England at one time, and in Spain at one time, almost the entire poetic imagination of the country found expression in the acted drama alone, is sufficient to show that a poet's artistic methods are very largely influenced by the artistic environments of his country and time. So vast a subject as this, however, is beyond our scope, and we can only point to the familiar instance of the troubadours and the trouvères and then pass on.

With the trouvère (the poet of the langue d'oil), the story or situation is always the end of which the musical language is the means ; with the troubadour (the poet of the langue d'oc), the form is so beloved, the musical language so enthralling, that, however beautiful may be the story or situation, it is felt to be no more than the means to a more beloved and beautiful end. But then nature makes her own troubadours, and her own trouvères irrespective of fashion and of time—irrespective of langue d'oc and langue d'oil. In comparing the troubadours with the trouvères, this is what strikes us at once—there are certain troubadours who by temperament, by original endowment of nature, ought to have been trouvères, and there are certain trouvères who by temperament ought to have been troubadours. Surrounding conditions alone have made them what they are. There are those whose impulse (though writing in obedience to contemporary fashions lyrics in the langue d'oc) is manifestly to narrate, and there are those whose impulse (though writing in obedience to contemporary fashions *fabliaux* in the langue d'oil) is simply to sing.

In other words, there are those who, though writing after the fashion of their brother-troubadours, are more impressed with the romance and wonderfulness of the human life outside them than with the romance and wonderfulness of their own passions, and who delight in depicting the external world in any form that may be the popular form of their time ; and there are those who, though writing after the fashion of their brother-trouvères, are far more occupied with the life within them than with that outer life which the taste of their time and country calls upon them to paint—born rhythmists who must sing, who translate everything external as well as internal into verbal melody. Of the former class Pierre Vidal, of the latter class the author of " Le Lay de l'Oiselet," may be taken as the respective types.

That the same forces are seen at work in all literatures few students of poetry will deny,—though in some poetical groups these forces are no doubt more potent than in others, as, for instance, with the great parable poets of Persia, in some of whom there is perpetually apparent a conflict between the dominance of the Oriental taste for allegory and subtle suggestion, as expressed in the Zoroastrian definition of poetry,—" apparent pictures of unapparent realities,"—and the opposite yearning to represent human life with the freshness and natural freedom characteristic of Western poetry.

Allowing, however, for all the potency of external influences, we shall not be wrong in saying that of poetic imagination there are two distinct kinds.

(1) the kind of poetic imagination seen at its highest in Æschylus, Sophocles, Shakespeare, and Homer, and

(2) the kind of poetic imagination seen at its highest in Pindar, Dante, and Milton, or else in Sappho, Heine, and Shelley.

The former, being in its highest dramatic exercise unconditioned by the personal or lyrical impulse of the poet, might perhaps be called absolute dramatic vision ; the latter, being more or less conditioned by the personal or lyrical impulse of the poet, might be called relative dramatic vision.   It seems impossible to classify poets, or to classify the different varieties of poetry, without drawing some such distinction as this, whatever words of definition we may choose to adopt.

For the achievement of all pure lyric poetry,

such as the ode, the song, the elegy, the idyl,
the sonnet, the stornello, it is evident that the
imaginative force we have called relative vision
will suffice. And if we consider the matter
thoroughly, in many other forms of poetic
art—forms which at first sight might seem to
require absolute vision—we shall find nothing
but relative vision at work.

Even in Dante, and even in Milton and Virgil,
it might be difficult to trace the working of any
other than relative vision. And as to the
entire body of Asiatic poets it might perhaps
be found (even in view of the Indian drama)
that relative vision suffices to do all their work.
Indeed the temper which produces true drama
is, it might almost be said, a growth of the
Western mind. For, unless it be Semitic as
seen in the dramatic narratives of the Bible,
or Chinese as seen in that remarkable prose
story, " The Two Fair Cousins," translated by
Remusat, absolute vision seems to have but
small place in the literatures of Asia.

The wonderfulness of the world and the
romantic possibilities of fate, or circumstance,
or chance—not the wonderfulness of the character to whom these possibilities befall—are
ever present to the mind of the Asiatic poet.

Even in so late a writer as the poet of the Shah Nameh, the hero Irij, the hero Zal, and the hero Zohreb, are in character the same person, the virtuous young man who combines the courage of youth with the wisdom and forbearance of age.   And, as regards the earlier poets of Asia, it was not till the shadowy demigods and heroes of the Asiatic races crossed the Caucasus, and breathed a more bracing air, that they became really individual characters.

But among the many qualities of man's mind that were invigorated and rejuvenated by that great exodus from the dreamy plains of Asia is to be counted, above all others, his poetic imagination.   The mere sense of wonder, which had formerly been an all-sufficing source of pleasure to him, was all-sufficing no longer. The wonderful adventure must now be connected with a real and interesting individual character.   It was left for the poets of Europe to show that, given the interesting character, given the Achilles, the Odysseus, the Helen, the Priam, any adventure happening to such a character becomes interesting.

What then is this absolute vision, this true dramatic imagination which can hardly be found in Asia—which even in Europe cannot **be found except in rare cases ?**

Between relative and absolute vision the difference seems to be this, that the former only enables the poet, even in its very highest exercise, to make his own individuality, or else humanity as represented by his own individuality, live in the imagined situation; the latter enables him in its highest exercise to make special individual characters other than the poet's own, live in the imagined situation.

" That which exists in nature," says Hegel, " is a something purely individual and particular. Art on the contrary is essentially destined to manifest the general." And no doubt this is true as regards the plastic arts, and true also as regards literary art, save in the very highest reaches of pure drama and pure lyric, when it seems to become art no longer—when it seems to become the very voice of Nature herself. The cry of Priam when he puts to his lips the hand that slew his son is not merely the cry of a bereaved and aged parent; it is the cry of the individual King of Troy, and expresses above everything else that most naïf, pathetic and winsome character. Put the words into the mouth of an irascible and passionate Lear and they would be entirely out of keeping.

It may be said then that, while the poet of

relative vision, even in its very highest exercise, can only, when depicting the external world, deal with the general, the poet of absolute vision can compete with Nature herself, and deal with both general and particular. If this is really so we may perhaps find a basis for a classification of poetry and poets. That all poets must be singers has already been maintained. But singers seem to be divisible into three classes :—First, the pure lyrists, each of whom can with his one voice sing only one tune ; secondly, the epic poets, save Homer, the bulk of the narrative poets, and the quasi-dramatists, each of whom can with his one voice sing several tunes ; and, thirdly, the true dramatists, who, having, like the nightingale of Gongora, many tongues, can sing all tunes.

It is to the first-named of these classes that most poets belong. With regard to the second-class, there are not of course many poets left for it ; the first absorbs so many. But, when we come to consider that among those who, with each his one voice, can sing many tunes, are Pindar, Firdausi, Jami, Virgil, Dante, Milton, Spenser, Goethe, Byron, Coleridge, Shelley, Keats, Schiller, Victor Hugo, the second-class is so various that no generalization save such a broad one as ours could embrace its members. And now we come to class three, and must pause. The third class is necessarily very small. In it can only be placed such names as Shakespeare, Æschylus, Sophocles, Homer, and (hardly) Chaucer.

These three kinds of poets represent three totally different kinds of poetic activity.

With regard to the first, the pure lyrists, the impulse is pure egoism. Many of them have less of even relative vision at its highest than the mass of mankind. They are often too much engaged with the emotions within to have any deep sympathy with the life around them. Of every poet of this class it may be said that his mind to him " a kingdom is," and that the smaller the poet the bigger to him is that kingdom. To make use of a homely image— like the chaffinch whose eyes have been pricked by the bird-fancier, the pure lyrist is sometimes a warbler because he is blind. Still he feels that the Muse loves him exceedingly. She takes away his eyesight, but she gives him sweet song. And his song is very sweet, very sad, and very beautiful ; but it is all about the world within his own soul—its sorrows, joys, fears, and aspirations.

With regard to the second class the impulse here is no doubt a kind of egoism too, yet the poets of this class are all of a different temper from the pure lyrists. They have a wide imagination, but it is still relative, still egoistic. They have splendid eyes, but eyes that never get beyond seeing general, universal humanity (typified by themselves) in the imagined situation. Not even to these is it given to break through that law of centrality by which every " me " feels itself to be the central " me."—the only " me " of the universe, round which all other spurious " me's " revolve. This " me " of theirs they can transmute into many shapes, but they cannot create other " me's,"—nay, for egoism, some of them scarcely would perhaps if they could.

The third class, the true dramatists, whose impulse is the simple yearning to create akin to that which made " the great Vishnu yearn to create a world," are " of imagination all compact "—so much so that when at work " the divinity " which Iamblichus speaks of " seizes for the time the soul, and guides it as he will."

The distinction between the pure lyrists and the other two classes of poets is obvious enough.

But the distinction between the quasi-dramatists and the pure dramatists requires a word
of explanation before we proceed to touch upon
the various kinds of poetry that spring from the
exercise of relative and absolute vision. Sometimes, to be sure, the vision of the true dramatists—the greatest dramatists—will suddenly
become narrowed and obscured, as in that part
of the *Œdipus Tyrannus* where Sophocles makes
Œdipus ignorant of what every one in Thebes
must have known, the murder of Laius. And,
again, finely as Sophocles has conceived the
character of Electra, he makes her, in her
dispute with Chrysothemis, give expression to
sentiments that, in another play of his own,
come far more appropriately from the lofty
character of Antigone in a parallel dispute with
Ismene. And, on the other hand, examples of
relative vision, in its furthest reaches, can be
found in abundance everywhere, especially in
Virgil, Dante, Calderon, and Milton. Some of
the most remarkable examples of that high
kind of relative vision which may easily be
mistaken for absolute vision may be found in
those great prose epics of the North, which
Aristotle would have called poems. Here is
one from the Völsunga Saga. While the brothers

of Gudrun are about their treacherous business
of murdering Sigurd, her husband, as he lies
asleep in her arms, Brynhild, Sigurd's former
love, who in the frenzy of " love turned to hate "
has instigated the murderers to the deed, hovers
outside the chamber with Gunnar, her husband,
and listens to the wail of her rival who is
weltering in Sigurd's blood. At the sound of
that wail Brynhild laughs.

> " Then said Gunnar to her : Thou laughest not because
> thy heart roots are gladded, *or else why doth thy visage
> wax so wan ?* " *

This is, of course, very fine ; but, as any two
characters in that dramatic situation might have
done that dramatic business, fine as it is—as
the sagaman gives us the general and not the
particular,—the vision at work is not absolute
but relative at its very highest exercise. But
our examples will be more interesting if taken
from English poets. In Coleridge's " Ancient
Mariner " we find an immense amount of
relative vision of so high a kind that at first
it seems absolute vision. When the ancient
mariner, in his narrative to the wedding guest,
reaches the slaying of the albatross, he stops,

*Translation of Morris and Magnusson

he can proceed no further, and the wedding guest exclaims :—

" God save thee, Ancient Mariner,
From the fiends that plague thee thus !
Why look'st thou so ? "   " With my cross-bow
I shot the albatross."

But there are instances of relative vision—especially in the great master of absolute vision, Shakespeare—which are higher still,—so high indeed that not to relegate them to absolute vision seems at first sight pedantic. Such an example is the famous speech of Lady Macbeth in the second act, where she says :—

" Had he not resembled
My father as he slept, I had done't."

Marvellously subtle as is this speech, it will be found, if analysed, that it expresses the general human soul rather than any one special human soul. Indeed, Leigh Hunt records the case of a bargeman who, charged with robbing a sleeping traveller in his barge, used in his confession almost identical words—" Had he not looked like my father as he slept, I should have killed as well as robbed him." Again, the thousand and one cases (to be found in every literature) where a character, overwhelmed by some sudden surprise or terror, asks whether the action going on is that of a dream or of real life, must all, on severe analysis, be classed under relative rather than under absolute vision, —even such a fine speech, for instance, as that where Pericles, on discovering Marina, exclaims :

> " This is the rarest dream that e'er dull sleep
> Did mock sad fools withal."

or as that in the third act of Titus Andronicus, where Titus, beholding his mutilated and ruined daughter, asks—

> " When will this fearful slumber have an end ? "

Even here, we say, the humanity rendered is general and not particular, the vision at work is relative and not absolute. The poet, as representing the whole human race, throwing himself into the imagined situation, gives us what general humanity would have thought, felt, said or done in that situation, not what one particular individual and he alone would have thought, felt, said, or done.

Now what we have called absolute vision operates in a very different way. So vividly is the poet's mere creative instinct at work

that the ego sinks into passivity—becomes
insensitive to all impressions other than those
dictated by the vision—by the " divinity "
which has " seized the soul."

Shakespeare is full of examples. Take the
scene in the first act of *Hamlet*, where Hamlet
hears for the first time, from Horatio, that his
father's ghost haunts the castle. Having by
short sharp questions elicited the salient facts
attending the apparition, Hamlet says, " I
would I had been there." To this Horatio
makes the very commonplace reply, " It would
have much amazed you." Note the marvellously dramatic reply of Hamlet—" Very
like, very like ! stayed it long ? " Suppose that
this dialogue had been attempted by any other
poet than a true dramatist, or by a true dramatist in any other mood than his very highest,
Hamlet, on hearing Horatio's commonplace
remarks upon phenomena, which to Hamlet
were more subversive of the very order of the
universe than if a dozen stars had fallen from
their courses, would have burst out with—
" Amazed me ! " and then would have followed
an eloquent declamation about the " amazing "
nature of the phenomena and their effect upon
him. But so entirely has the poet become

Hamlet, so completely has " the divinity seized his soul," that all language seems equally weak for expressing the turbulence within the soul of the character, and Hamlet exclaims in a sort of meditative irony, " Very like, very like ! " It is exactly this one man Hamlet, and no other man, who in this situation would have so expressed himself.

Charles Knight has some pertinent remarks upon this speech of Hamlet ; yet he misses its true value and treats it from the general rather than from the particular side. Instances of absolute vision in Shakespeare crowd upon us ; but we can find room for only one other. In the pathetic speech of Othello, just before he kills himself, he declares himself to be :

> " One not easily jealous, but, being *wrought*,
>   Perplexed in the extreme."

Consider the marvellous *timbre* of the word " wrought " as coming from a character like Othello. When writing this passage, especially when writing this word, the poet had become entirely the simple English soldier-hero, as the Moor really is—he had become Othello, look-ing upon himself as " not easily jealous," whereas he was " wrought " and " perplexed in the extreme " by tricks which Hamlet would have seen through in a moment.

Victor Hugo furnishes two striking examples of what we mean by lyric imagination and dramatic imagination. In the one he makes pure fancy do the work of dramatic imagination. We allude to the passage in the second series of " La Légende des Siècles," where he calls up the picture of the crescent moon hanging over the lonely sea :

> " Ce fer d'or qu'a laissé tomber dans les nuées
> Le sombre cheval de la nuit ? "

The other occurs in the first series where, watching Boaz asleep, and looking across him over the harvest-field, Ruth, on seeing the crescent moon bent among the stars, asks herself :

> " Quel dieu, quel moissonneur de l'éternal été
> Avait, en s'en allant, négligemment jeté,
> Cette faucelle d'or dans le champ des étoiles ?

It would be difficult to find a finer example of dramatic imagination than this. The poet has entered the soul of Ruth.

While all other forms of poetic art can be vitalized by relative vision, there are two forms (and these the greatest) in which absolute vision is demanded, viz., the drama, and in a lesser degree the Greek epic, especially the Iliad. This will be seen more plainly perhaps if we now vary our definitions and call relative vision egoistic imagination, absolute vision dramatic imagination.

It is not within the scope of this work to discuss in detail the vast subject of drama, which would require a book by itself ; but inferentially we have been able to say much that will convey our generalizations upon the subject.

Much of the dramatist's work can be, and in fact is, effected by egoistic imagination, while true dramatic imagination is only called into play on comparatively rare occasions. Not only fine but sublime dramatic poems have been written, however, where the vitalizing power has been entirely that of lyrical imagination. We need only instance the *Prometheus Bound* of Æschylus, the most sublime poem in the world. The dramas of Shelley too, like those of Victor Hugo and Calderon, are informed entirely by egoistic imagination. In all these splendid poems the dramatist places himself in the imagined situation, or at most he places there some typical conception of universal humanity.

There is not in all Calderon any such display of dramatic imagination as we get in that wonderful speech of Priam's in the last book of the Iliad to which we have before alluded.

There is not in the Cenci such a display of dramatic imagination as we get in the sudden burst of anger from the spoilt child of gods and men, Achilles (anger which alarms the hero himself as much as it alarms Priam), when the prattle of the old man has carried him too far. It may seem bold to say that the drama of Goethe is informed by egoistic imagination only—assuredly the prison-scene in *Faust* is unsurpassed in the literatures of the world. Yet, perhaps, it could be shown of the passion and the pathos of Gretchen throughout the entire play that it betrays a female character general and typical rather than individual and particular.

The nature of this absolute vision or true dramatic imagination is easily seen if we compare the dramatic work of writers without absolute vision, such as Calderon, Goethe, Ben Jonson, Fletcher, and others, with the dramatic work of Æschylus and of Shakespeare. While of the former group it may be said that each poet skilfully works his imagination, of Æschylus and Shakespeare it must be said that each in his highest dramatic mood does not work, but is worked by his imagination. Note, for instance, how the character of Clytæmnestra grows and glows under the hand of Æschylus.

The poet of the Odyssey had distinctly said that Ægisthus, her paramour, had struck the blow, but the dramatist, having imagined the greatest tragic female in all poetry, finds it impossible to let a man like Ægisthus assist such a woman in a homicide so daring and so momentous. And when in that terrible speech of hers she justifies her crime (ostensibly to the outer world, but really to her own conscience) the way in which, by the sheer magnetism of irresistible personality, she draws our sympathy to herself, and her crime is unrivalled out of Shakespeare and not surpassed even there. In the Great Drama, in the Agamemnon, in Othello, in Hamlet, in Macbeth, there is an imagination at work whose laws are inexorable, are inevitable, as the laws by the operation of which the planets move around the sun.

Considering how large and on the whole how good is the body of modern criticism upon drama, it is surprising how poor is the modern criticism upon epic. Aristotle, comparing tragedy with epic, gives the palm to tragedy as being the more perfect art, and nothing can be more ingenious than the way in which he has marshalled his reasons. He tells as that tragedy as well as epic is capable of producing its effect even without action ; we can judge of it perfectly, says he, by reading. He goes so far as to say that, even in reading as well as in representation, tragedy has an advantage over the epic, the advantage of greater clearness and distinctness of impression. And in some measure this was perhaps true of Greek tragedy, for as Müller in his *Dissertations on the Eumenides* has well said, the ancients always remained and wished to remain conscious that the whole was a Dionysian entertainment ; the quest of a commonplace ἀπάτη came afterwards. And even of of Romantic Drama it may be said that in the time of Shakespeare, and indeed down through the eighteenth century, it never lost entirely its character of a recitation as well as a drama. It was not till melodrama began to be recognised as a legitimate form of dramatic art that the dialogue had to be struck from the dramatic action " at full speed "—struck like sparks from the roadster's shoes. The truth is, however, that it was idle for Aristotle to inquire which is the more important branch of poetry, epic or tragedy.

Equally idle would it be for the modern critic to inquire how much romantic drama gained and how much it lost by abandoning the chorus. Much has been said as to the scope and the limits of epic and dramatic poetry. If in epic the poet has the power to take the imagination of his audience away from the dramatic centre and show what is going on at the other end of the great web of the world, he can do the same thing in drama by the chorus, and also by the introduction into the dramatic circle of messengers and others from the outside world.

But as regards epic poetry, is it right that we should hear, as we sometimes do hear, the voice of the poet himself as chorus bidding us contrast the present picture with other pictures afar off, in order to enforce its teaching and illustrate its pathos ?   This is a favourite method with modern poets and a still more favourite one with prose narrators. Does it not give an air of self-consciousness to poetry ? Does it not disturb the intensity of the poetic vision ? Yet it has the sanction of Homer ; and who shall dare to challenge the methods of the great father of epic ?   An instance occurs in Iliad v. where, in the midst of all the stress of fight, the poet leaves the dramatic action to tell us what became of the inheritance of Phænops after his two sons had been slain by Diomedes.

The only other instance occurs in iii. 243-4, where the poet, after Helen's pathetic mention of her brothers, comments on the causes of their absence, generalizes upon the impotence of human intelligence—the impotence even of human love—to pierce the darkness in which the web of human fate is woven. Thus she spoke (the poet tells us) ; but the life-giving earth already possessed them, there in Lacedæmon, in their dear native land :—

ὣς φάτο τοὺς δ'ἤδη κάτεχεν φυσίροος αια
ἐν Λακεδαίμονι αὖθι φίλῃ ἐν πατρίδι γαίῃ.

This, of course, is " beautiful exceedingly," but, inasmuch as the imagination at work is egoistic or lyrical, not dramatic, inasmuch as the vision is relative not absolute, it does not represent that epic strength at its very highest which we call specially " Homeric," unless indeed we remember that with Homer the Muses are omniscient ; this certainly may give the passage a deep dramatic value it otherwise seems to lack.

The deepest of all the distinctions between dramatic and epic methods has relation, however, to the nature of the dialogue. Aristotle failed to point it out, and this is remarkable until we remember that his work is but a fragment of a great system of criticism. In epic poetry, and in all poetry that narrates, whether the poet be Homer, Chaucer, Thomas the Rhymer, Gottfried von Strasburg, or Turoldus, the action, of course, moves by aid partly of narrative and partly by aid of dialogue, but in drama the dialogue has a quality of suggestiveness and subtle inference which we do not expect to find in any other poetic form save perhaps that of the purely dramatic ballad.

In ancient drama this quality of suggestiveness and subtle inference is seen not only in the dialogue, but in the choral odes. The third ode of the *Agamemnon* is an extreme case in point, where, by a kind of *double entendre*, the relations of Clytæmnestra and Ægisthus are darkly alluded to under cover of allusions to Paris and Helen. Of this dramatic subtlety Sophocles is perhaps the greatest master ; and certain critics have been led to speak as though irony were the heart-thought of Sophoclean drama. But the suggestiveness of Sophocles is pathetic (as the late Prof. Lewis Campbell has well pointed out) not ironical. This is one reason why drama more than epic seems to satisfy the mere intellect of the reader, though this may be counterbalanced by the hardness of mechanical structure which sometimes disturbs the reader's imagination in tragedy.

When, for instance, a dramatist pays so much attention to the evolution of the plot as Sophocles does, it is inevitable that his characters should be more or less plot-ridden ; they have to say and do now and then certain things which they would not say and do but for the exigencies of the plot. Indeed one of the advantages which epic certainly has over drama is that the story can be made to move as rapidly as the poet may desire without these mechanical modifications of character.

With regard to the difference between epic and drama, the late Leslie Stephen has made some admirable remarks upon this subject. "A play may be read as well as seen," he says, "but it calls for an effort of imagination on the part of the reader which can never quite supply the place of actual sight ; and the play intended only for the study becomes simply a novel told in a clumsy method."

The artistic question raised in this passage is a certain answer to Aristotle. Aristotle, as we have seen, decided in favour of dramatic as against narrative art, on the ground that a play can be both read and seen. But then Aristotle's idea of a play was very different from the modern idea of dramatic art. Narrative pure and simple formed a very large portion of a Greek play. Indeed, in one of the tragedies of Æschylus, the ' Septem contra Thebas,' the messenger's narrative and enumeration of the allied chiefs, in about three hundred lines or more, forms something like a third part of the play, while a modern drama, even by an Elizabethan, consists of dialogue struck rigidly from the action. Still the drama of the Elizabethans was a flexible form of art. It gave the dramatist sufficient room and freedom not only to depict his characters, but to develop them before the eyes of the audience, not so fully, indeed, as characters can be developed in prose fiction, but still with an almost sufficient fulness. If the exigencies of the contemporary stage are such that the dramatist can do this no longer, while the writers of plays to be read *must* do it in order to achieve anything like worthy work, then the difference between the acted and the unacted drama is so wide that they can hardly be placed in the same category. This being so, is or is not the mechanical scaffolding of a play an encumbrance to the writer, and an impediment to the movement of the reader's imagination ? Without attempting to decide upon the point, we may at least say this, that a form of art which at certain periods and in certain countries is flexible may become inflexible at certain other periods and in certain other countries ; and that the moment a form of art has lost its flexibility—lost that power which should enable it to give a vital picture of the time—it ceases to be a good literary form, and there is no need to try to kill it, it will die a natural death.

Much has been written about the severance in our time between the acted drama and dramatic poetry. That the growth of realism in art is a necessary and inevitable result of that complexity, and that searching knowingness of temper, which belong to a social arrangement like that of modern times is true. It is true, too, that in the drama especially the demand of spectators for further and still further material illusion makes it at last necessary that every speech shall have a theatric *raison d'être*, and almost even a spectacular one—that every response, in short, shall be struck from the dramatic action, so to speak, as the spark is struck from the flint and steel. And this being so, a closet play or unacted drama seems to be the only form of poetic art still remaining in which the poet is able to develop in pure poetic forms his conception of a subtle and complex character, as he would in the time of Shakespeare have developed it in an acting play.

But having determined to produce a drama not for the boards, but for the closet, there arises the important question how far the poet may legitimately free himself from those theatric conditions which, being incidents of the modern type of acted drama, are really incidents of a form of art different from that which he is attempting ; for it must be borne in mind that the points which aid illusion in the contemporary theatre tend not to aid but to destroy illusion in the closet. Take, for instance, such a drama as the late Lord Lytton's "Lady of Lyons," and, again, take "Philip Van Artevelde" or Swinburne's "Bothwell." In the first case so skilfully is the dialogue elicited by the theatric situation that its utter falsity to nature is forgotten by the spectator; while in the other two plays dialogue, which is so true to nature and to the actual facts of history as to produce when read something of the illusion of a contemporary chronicle is so little supported by theatric conditions that "Philip Van Artevelde," even after much pruning, does not act well, while "Bothwell" could never be acted at all. A single act of thirteen scenes, and a speech of several hundred verses have been called monstrous, and, indeed, are monstrous in a tragedy. Yet it is, perhaps, a mere question of names after all. Had these plays been called simply, "dramatic chronicles," the reply to objectors against their great length and defective construction would be by a question, What, then, is the proper construction, and what is the proper length of a dramatic chronicle? Clearly, therefore, there is very great freedom of construction allowed to the writer of a modern closet play. Yet the laws of imaginative art are here not less inexorable than they were in an acted drama, but more so. The more entirely free is the closet drama from the conditions of theatrical illusion, the less free is it to dispense with poetic illusion, i.e. with that dramatic truth which the spectacular realism of the theatre can alone cause us to dispense with and forget,

"Because things seen are mightier than things heard."

The only kind of epic for Aristotle to consider was Greek epic, between which and all other epic the difference is one of kind, if the Iliad alone is taken to represent Greek epic. In speaking of the effect that surrounding conditions seem to have upon the form in which the poetic energy of any time or country should express itself, we instanced the Iliad as a typical case. The imagination vivifying it is mainly dramatic. The characters represent much more than the mere variety of mood of the delineator. Notwithstanding all the splendid works of Calderon, Marlowe, Webster and Goethe, it is doubtful whether as a born dramatist the poet of the Iliad does not come nearer to Æschylus and Shakespeare than does any other poet. His passion for making the heroes speak for themselves is almost a fault in the Iliad considered as pure epic, and the unconscious way in which each actor is made to depict his own character is in the highest spirit of drama.

It is owing to this speciality of the Iliad that it stands apart from all other epic save that of the Odyssey, where, however, the dramatic vision is less vivid. It is owing to the dramatic imagination displayed in the Iliad that it is impossible to say, from internal evidence, whether the poem is to be classified with the epics of growth or with the epics of art.

In poetic art the more Homerically the great fundamental passions of man's nature are treated, that is to say, the more simply and singly, the more powerful is the effect. Shakespeare is so alive to this great law of the human mind that he sometimes misses an easy and obvious method of lending verisimilitude to a situation rather than vex his audience with a multiplicity of motives, as in the relations between Lear and Cordelia, where it would have been easy to clear the old king from the obvious charge of fatuity by making him to.be hoodwinked as to Cordelia's real affection by some well-devised plot of Goneril and Regan.

All epics are clearly divisible into two classes, first those which are a mere accretion of poems or traditionary ballads, and second, those which, though based indeed on tradition or history, have become so fused in the mind of one great poet, so stained, therefore, with the colour and temper of that mind, as to become new crystallizations—inventions, in short, as we understand that word. Each kind of epic has excellencies peculiar to itself, accompanied by peculiar and indeed necessary defects. In the one we get the freedom—apparently schemeless and motiveless—of nature, but, as a conse-

quence, miss that "hard acorn of thought"
(to use the picturesque definition in the Völsunga Saga of the heart of a man) which the
mind asks for as the core of every work of art.
In the other this great requisite of an adequate
central thought is found, but accompanied by a
constriction, a lack of freedom, a cold artificiality
the obtrusion of a pedantic scheme, which would
be intolerable to the natural mind unsophisti-
cated by literary study. The flow of the one is
as that of a river, the flow of the other as that
of a canal. Yet, as has been already hinted,
though the great charm of Nature herself is
that she never teases us with any obtrusive
exhibitions of scheme, she doubtless has a
scheme somewhere, she does somewhere hide a
" hard acorn of thought" of which the poem
of the universe is the expanded expression.
And, this being so, art should have a scheme
too ; but in such a dilemma is she placed in this
matter that the epic poet, unless he is evidently
telling the story for its own sake, scornful of
purposes ethic or æsthetic, must sacrifice illusion.

Among the former class of epics are to be
placed the great epics of growth such as the
Mahâbhârata, the Niblung story, &c.; among
the latter the Odyssey, the Æneid, Paradise

Lost, the Gerusalemme Liberata, the Lusiadas.

But where in this classification are we to find a place for the Iliad ? The heart-thought of the greatest epic in all literature is simply that Achilles was vexed, and that the fortunes of the world depended upon the whim of a sulky hero. Yet, notwithstanding all the acute criticisms of Wolff, it remains difficult for us to find a place for the Iliad among the epics of growth. And why ? Because throughout the Iliad the dramatic imagination shown is of the first order ; and, if we are to suppose a multiplicity of authors for the poem, we must also suppose that ages before the time of Pericles there existed a group of dramatists more nearly akin to the masters of the great drama, Æschylus, Sophocles, and Shakespeare than any group that has ever existed since. Yet it is equally difficult to find a place for it amongst the epics of art. In the matter of artistic motive the Odyssey stands alone among the epics of art of the world, as we are going to see.

It is manifest that, as the pleasure derived from the epic of art is that of recognizing a conscious scheme, if the epic of art fails through confusion of scheme it fails altogether. What is demanded of the epic of art (as some kind of compensation for that natural freedom of evolution which it can never achieve, that sweet *abandon* which belongs to nature and to the epic of growth alike) is unity of impression, harmonious and symmetrical development of a conscious heart-thought or motive. This being so, where are we to place the Æneid, and where are we to place the Shah Nameh ? Starting with the intention, as it seems, of fusing into one harmonious whole the myths and legends upon which the Roman story is based, Virgil, by the time he reaches the middle of his epic, forgets all about this primary intent, and gives us his own thoughts and reflexions on things in general. Fine as is the speech of Anchises to Æneas in Elysium (Æn. vi. 724-755), its incongruity with the general scheme of the poem as developed in the previous books shows how entirely Virgil lacked that artistic power shown in the Odyssey of making a story become the natural and inevitable outcome of an artistic idea.

In the *Shah Nameh*, there is the artistic redaction of Virgil, but with even less attention to a central thought than Virgil exhibits. Firdausi relies for his effects upon the very qualities which characterize not the epic of art, but the epic of growth—a natural and not an artificial flow of the story ; so much so indeed that, if the *Shah Nameh* were studied in connexion with the *Iliad* on the one hand, and with the *Kalevala* on the other, it might throw a light upon the way in which an epic may be at one and the same time an aggregation of the national ballad poems and the work of a single artificer. That Firdausi was capable of working from a centre not only artistic but philosophic his *Yusuf and Zuleikha* shows ; and if we consider what was the artistic temper of the Persians in Firdausi's time, what indeed has been the temper during the whole of the Mohammedan period, the subtle temper of the parable poet,—the *Shah Nameh*, with its direct appeal to popular sympathies, is a standing wonder in poetic literature.

With regard, however, to Virgil's defective power of working from an artistic motive, as compared with the poet of the *Odyssey*, this is an infirmity he shares with all the poets of the western world. Certainly he shares it with the writer of *Paradise Lost*, who, setting out to " justify the ways of God to man," forgets occasionally the original worker of the evil, as where, for instance, he substitutes chance as soon as he comes (at the end of the second book) to the point upon which the entire epic movement turns, the escape of Satan from hell and his journey to earth for the ruin of man :—

> " At last his sail-broad vans
> He spreads for flight, and, in the surging smoke
> Uplifted, spurns the ground ; thence many a league,
> As in a cloudy chair, ascending rides
> Audacious, but, that seat soon failing, meets
> A vast vacuity ; all unawares,
> Fluttering his pinions vain, plumb down he drops
> Ten thousand fathoms deep, and to this hour
> Down had been falling, had not, by *ill chance*,
> The strong rebuff of some tumultuous cloud,
> Instinct with fire and nitre, hurried him
> As many miles aloft."

In Milton's case, however, the truth is that he made the mistake of trying to disturb the motive of a story for artistic purposes—a fatal mistake as we shall see when we come to speak of the *Nibelungenlied* in relation to the old Norse epic cycle.

Though Vondel's mystery play of *Lucifer* is, in its execution, rhetorical more than poetical, it did, beyond all question influence Milton when he came to write *Paradise Lost*. The famous line which is generally quoted as the key-note of Satan's character :—

> " Better to reign in hell than serve in heaven."

seems to have been taken bodily from Vondel's play, and Milton's entire epic shows a study of it. While Marlowe's majestic movements alone are traceable in Satan's speech (written some years before the rest of *Paradise Lost*, when the dramatic and not the epic form had been selected), Milton's Satan became afterwards a splendid amalgam not of the Mephistopheles, but of the *Faustus* of Marlowe and the *Lucifer* of Vondel. Vondel's play must have possessed a peculiar attraction for a poet of Milton's views of human progress. Defective as the play is in execution, it is far otherwise in motive. This motive, if we consider it aright, is nothing less than an explanation of man's anomalous condition on the earth—spirit incarnate in matter, created by God, a little lower than the angels—in order that he may advance by means of these very manacles which imprison him, in order that he may ascend by the staircase of the world, the ladder of fleshly conditions, above those cherubim and seraphim who, lacking the education of sense, have not the knowledge wide and deep which brings men close to God.

Here Milton found his own favourite doctrine of human development and self-education in a concrete and vividly artistic form. Much, however, as such a motive must have struck a man of Milton's instincts, his intellect was too much chained by Calvinism to permit of his treating the subject with Vondel's philosophic breadth. The cause of Lucifer's wrath had to be changed from jealousy of human progress to jealousy of the son's proclaimed superiority. And the history of poetry shows that once begin to tamper with the central thought around which any group of incidents has crystallized, and the entire story becomes thereby re-written, as we have seen in the case of the *Agamemnon* of Æschylus. Of the motive of his own epic, after he had abandoned the motive of Vondel, Milton had as little permanent grasp as Virgil had of his. As regards the *Odyssey*, however, we need scarcely say that its motive is merely artistic, not philosophic. And now we come to philosophic motive.

The artist's power of thought is properly shown not in the direct enunciation of ideas, but in mastery over motive. Here Æschylus is by far the greatest figure in Western poetry —a proof, perhaps, among many proofs of the Oriental strain of his genius. (As regards pure drama, however, important as is motive, freedom, organic vitality in every part, is of more importance than even motive, and in this freedom and easy abandonment the concluding part of the *Oresteia* is deficient as compared with such a play as *Othello* or *Lear*). Notwithstanding the splendid exception of Æschylus, the truth seems to be that the faculty of developing a poetical narrative from a philosophic thought is Oriental, and on the whole foreign to the genius of the Western mind. Neither in Western drama nor in Western epic do we find, save in such rare cases as that of Vondel, anything like that power of developing a story from an idea which not only Jami, but all the parable poets of Persia show.

In recent English poetry, the motive of Shelley's dramatic poem *Prometheus Unbound* is a notable illustration of what is here contended. Starting with the full intent of developing a drama from a motive—starting with a universalism, a belief that good shall be the final goal of ill—Shelley cannot finish his first three hundred lines without shifting (in the curse of Prometheus) into a Manichæism as pure as that of Manes himself :—

> " Heap on thy soul, by virtue of this curse,
>   Ill deeds, then be thou damned, beholding good ;
> *Both* infinite as is the universe."

According to the central thought of the poem, human nature, through the heroic protest and struggle of the human mind typified by Prometheus, can at last dethrone that supernatural terror and tyranny (Jupiter) which the human mind had itself installed. But, after its dethronement (when human nature becomes infinitely perfectible), how can the super-natural tyranny exist apart from the human mind that imagined it ? How can it be as " infinite as the universe ? "

The motive of *Paradise Lost* is assailed with much vigour by Victor Hugo in his poem *Religions et Religion*. But when Hugo, in the after parts of the poem, having destroyed Milton's " God," sets up an entirely French " Dieu " of his own and tries " to justify " him, we perceive how pardonable was Milton's failure after all. Compare such defect of mental grip and such nebulosity of thought as is displayed by Milton, Shelley, and Hugo with the strength of hand shown in the " Sálámán " and " Absal " of Jami, and indeed by the Sufi poets generally.

There is, however, one exception to this rule that Western poetry is nebulous as to motive. There is, besides the Iliad, one epic that refuses to be classified, though for entirely different reasons. This is the Niblung story, where we find unity of purpose and also entire freedom of movement. We find combined here beauties which are nowhere else combined—which are, in fact, at war with each other everywhere else. We find a scheme, a real " acorn of thought " in an epic which is not the self-conscious work of a single poetic artificer, but is as much the slow growth of various times and various minds as is the Mahâbhârata, in which the heart-thought is merely that the Kauravas defeated their relatives at dice and refused to disgorge their winnings.

This Northern epic-tree, as we find it in the Icelandic sagas, the Norns themselves must have watered ; for it combines the virtues of the epic of growth with those of the epic of art. Though not written in metre, it may usefully be compared with the epics of Greece and of India and Persia. Free in movement as the wind, which " bloweth where it listeth," it listeth to move by law. Its action is that of free-will, but free-will at play within a ring of necessity. Within this ring there throbs all the warm and passionate life of the world outside, and all the freedom apparently. Yet from that world is enisled by a cordon of curses—by a zone of defiant flames more impregnable than that which girdled the beautiful Brynhild at Hindfell. Natural laws, familiar emotions, are at work everywhere in the story ; yet the ' Ring of Andvari," whose circumference is but that of a woman's finger, encircles the whole mimic world of the sagaman as the Midgard snake encircles the earth.

For this artistic perfection in an epic of growth there are, of course, many causes, some of them traceable, and some of them beyond all discovery—causes no doubt akin to those which gave birth to many of the beauties of other epics of growth. Originally Sinfiotli and Sigurd were the same person, and note how vast has been the artistic effect of the separation of the two ! Again, there were several different versions of the story of Brynhild. The sagamen, finding all these versions too interesting and too much beloved to be discarded, adopted them all—worked them up into one legend, so that, in the *Völsunga Saga* we have a heroine possessing all the charms of goddess, demi-goddess, earthly princess, and amazon—a heroine surpassing perhaps in fascination all other heroines that have ever figured in poetry.

It is when we come to consider such imagina-

tive work as this that we are compelled to pause
before challenging the Aristotelian doctrine that
metrical structure is but an accidental quality
of epic.

In speaking of the Niblung story we do not,
of course, speak of the German version, the
Nibelungenlied, a fine epic still, though a degradation of the elder form. Between the two
the differences are fundamental in the artistic
sense, and form an excellent illustration of what
has just been said upon the disturbance of
motive in epic, and indeed in all poetic art.
It is not merely that the endings of the three
principal characters Sigurd (Siegfried), Gudrun
(Kriemhilt), and Brynhild are entirely different ;
it is not merely that the Icelandic version, by
missing the blood-bath at Fafnir's lair, loses the
pathetic situation of Gudrun's becoming afterwards an unwilling instrument of her husband's
death ; it is not merely that, on the other hand,
the German version, by omitting the early love
passages between Brynhild and Sigurd at Hind-
fall, misses entirely the tragic meaning of her
story and the terrible hate that is love resulting
from the breaking of the troth ; but the conclusion of each version is so exactly the opposite
of that of the other that, while the German

story is called (and very properly) " Kriemhilt's Revenge," the story of the *Völsunga Saga* might, with equal propriety, be called Gudrun's Forgiveness.

If it be said that, in both cases, the motive shows the same Titanic temper, that is because the Titanic temper is the special characteristic of the North-Western mind. The temper of revolt against authority seems indeed to belong to that energy which succeeds in the modern development of the great racial struggle for life. Although no epic, Eastern or Western, can exist without a struggle between good and evil—and a struggle upon apparently equal terms—it must not be supposed that the warring of conflicting forces, which is the motive of the Eastern epic has much real relation to the warring of conflicting forces, which is the motive of Western epic.

And, as regards the machinery of epic, there is, we suspect, a deeper significance than is commonly apprehended in the fact that the Satan or Shaitàn of the Eastern world becomes in Vondel and Milton a sublime Titan who attracts to himself the admiration which in Eastern poetry belongs entirely to the authority of heaven. In Asia, save perhaps among the pure

Arabs of the desert, underlying all religious forms, there is apparent a temper of resignation to the irresistible authority of heaven. And as regards the Aryans it is probable that the Titanic temper—the temper of revolt against authority—did not begin to show itself till they had moved across the Caucasus. But what concerns us here is the fact that the farther they moved to the North west the more vigorously this temper asserted itself, the prouder grew man in his attitude towards the gods, till at last in the Scandinavian cycle he became their equal, and struggled alongside them, shoulder to shoulder, in the defence of heaven against the assaults of hell.

Therefore, as we say, the student of epic poetry must not suppose that there is any real parallel between the attitude of Vishnu (as Rama) towards Ravana and the attitude of Prometheus towards Zeus, or the attitude of the human heroes towards Odin in Scandinavian poetry. Had Ravana been clothed with a properly constituted authority, had he been a legitimate god instead of a demon, the Eastern doctrine of recognition of authority would most likely have come in, and the world would have been spared one at least of its enormous epics.

Indeed, the Ravana of the *Râmâyana* answers somewhat to the Fafnir of the *Völsunga Saga ;* and to plot against demons is not to rebel against authority. The vast field of Indian epic, however, is quite beyond us here.

Nor can we do more than glance at the *Kalevala.* From one point of view that group of ballads might be taken, no doubt, as a simple record of how the men of Kalevala were skilful in capturing the sisters of the Pojohla men. But from another point of view the universal struggle of the male for the female seems typified in this so-called epic of the Finns by the picture of the " Lady of the Rainbow " sitting upon her glowing arc, and weaving her golden threads, while the hero is doing battle with the malevolent forces of nature.

But it is in the Niblung story that the temper of Western epic is at its best—the temper of the simple fighter whose business is to fight. The ideal Western fighter was not known in Greece till ages after Homer, when in the pass of Thermopylæ the companions of Leonidas combed their long hair in the sun. The business of the fighter in Scandinavian epic is to yield to no power whatsoever, whether of earth, or heaven, or hell—to take a buffet from the All-father himself, and to return it ; to look Destiny herself in the face, crying out for quarter neither to gods nor demons, nor Norns.

This is the true temper of pure "heroic poetry" as it has hitherto flourished on this side of the Caucasus—the temper of the fighter who is invincible because he feels that Fate herself falters when the hero of the true strain defies—the fighter who feels that the very Norns themselves must cringe at last before the simple courage of man standing naked and bare of hope against all assaults whether of heaven or hell or doom. The proud heroes of the *Völsunga Saga* utter no moans and shed no Homeric tears, knowing as they know that the day prophesied is sure when, shoulder to shoulder, gods and men shall stand up to fight the entire brood of night and evil, storming the very gates of Asgard.

That this temper is not the highest from the ethical point of view is no doubt true. Against the beautiful resignation of Buddhism it may seem barbaric, and if moral suasion could supplant physical force in epic—if Siddartha could take the place of Achilles or Sigurd—it might be better for the human race.

Returning now to the general subject of

egoistic, or lyrical and dramatic imagination—
as might be expected, we occasionally meet
imagination of a purely dramatic kind in
narrative poetry, such for instance as that of
Gottfried von Strasburg, of Chaucer, and of the
author of the Chanson de Roland.

It is in the moulding of characters that the
narrative poet competes with the prose story-
teller. And here again Chaucer is the great
model. It is but natural that opinions should
greatly differ about his place among the highest
names.

If it be said of him that he has no prophetic
gift, that he is no seer, like Æschylus and Dante,
like Milton and Shelley, the impeachment cannot be answered, for it is true. May a poet lay
claim to a place in the first rank, and yet be
no seer ? There are poets who are organized to
see more clearly than we can ourselves see the
riches of the "world at hand"; do they rank
below those who are so dazzled by gazing above
it, and beyond it, that not only the flowers and
grass and trees of the earth, but even its men
and women, are common and superfluous ?

Of the simply terrene poets Chaucer is the
king. If health in poetry is the sweet acceptance and melodious utterance of the beauty of
the world as it is, Chaucer is the most healthy
poet that has appeared in any literature. His
delight is to represent.

Of all poets he is the most purely artistic ;
so that he can paint, for his own enjoyment and

ours, a beautiful picture, he cares not from
what source he draws his materials. The
riches and the wonderfulness of life—these are
his theme—a theme which is as fresh and delightful now as it was in his time, and as fresh
and delightful as it was when all those countless stories of romantic adventure upon which
his poetry and all the imaginative literature of
the West are built were lisped in the Aryan
cradle. Marlowe's "Hero and Leander" is a
splendid piece of narrative poetry, incompar-
ably finer than Shakespeare's "Venus and
Adonis," and shows yet another side of his
superb genius. A famous passage in Keats's
"Eve of St. Agnes" was certainly suggested by
Marlowe's couplet,

> "Mermaid-like, unto the floor she slid ;
> One half appeared—the other half was hid."

Character drawing in poetry as the result of
relative vision is no doubt the same as character
drawing in prose art.

The true artist is not he who paints exactly
what he sees, nor he whose sentimental, humorous, æsthetic, or ethical purpose is obtrusively
apparent ; but he who, while really fashioning
his characters out of broad general elements
from universal types of humanity—at the same
time deceives us into mistaking these characters
for real biographies—deceives us by appearing
(from his mastery over the properties of the
"fictionist") to be drawing from particulars—
from peculiar individual traits instead of from
generalities—and especially by never obtruding,

but rather by hiding away from us, all sentimental, humorous, æsthetic, or ethical purposes.

Chaucer is still perhaps our greatest narrative
poet. Scott is very great, but his lack of artistic
conscience damages and weakens his work.

It must be said of narrative poets generally
that they are apt to fail in " making their flats
join " to use a striking locution of the stage.
Victor Hugo, for instance, paints his flats most
brilliantly, but when he comes to put them
together, it is remarkable how clumsy his work
is. " La Légende des Siècles," for instance,
consists of a vast number of poems, having as
much connection with each other as " marbles
in a bag," to use Coleridge's expressive phrase.

" La Légende des Siècles " pretends to be
an epic of which a vast number of heterogeneous poems are thrown together.

The first series consisted of a collection of
detached scenes from history and legend (produced evidently at various times as the poet's
discursive reading suggested them), scenes
beginning with the birth of Eve's firstborn, and
ending with " La Trompette du Jugement."

The second series is more heterogeneous,
consisting of narrative, homily, lyric, satire,
drama—a collection for which an English poet
would have been quite unable to find any better
name than " Poems " or " Poems and Dramatic
Scenes," but for which the quick genius of a
countryman of Taine and the author of the
Comédie Humaine could easily find a more
ambitious title, having most likely " Dieu,"
" L'Ame," and " L'Homme," for the noun

substantives—a collection, in short, which Victor Hugo would naturally call " The Legend of the Ages."

The first volume of the second series opens with a poem, entitled " La Vision d'ou est sorti ce Livre," in which, as in the Preface to the first series, the poet endeavours to show that there is a great *idée mère* in these

> "Orient pearls at random strung."

Fortunately, however, as the reader goes on,— or, rather, is carried along,—breathless from beauty to beauty, from glory to glory, he finds to his delight that there is no such *idée mère* at all—nothing but poetry ; that there is no hint of that appalling " Fin de Satan " ; nothing to dread from " Dieu."

The power of thought in the artist is, of course, properly shown, not in ratiocination, but in the invention of *motif*. And Victor Hugo's " La Légende des Siècles " written under various impulses, and thrown together as recklessly, it would almost seem, as Shakespeare's sonnets— we are asked to accept, as embodying the greatest *motif* cognizable by the mind of man, or, rather, they are to be taken as part of the great embodiment ; for " La Légende des Siècles " is only part of an enormous epic of the Universe, of which " Dieu " is the protagonist and " L'Infini " the field of action.

Now it is just when we do come to consider these poems as integral parts of that vast organic whole,—of any organic whole; it is just when we do come to consider Victor Hugo's claims as a philosopher, who, looking over Past, Present, and Future, has something new to tell us about " Dieu," " La Fin de Satan," and the " Legend of Ages "—some explanation to offer us of " the painful riddle of the earth," of the wonder and the mystery of the human story—that we see how deficient is this great poet.

Unless the philosophic power of a poet is of the first order, so gigantic a conception as that of Victor Hugo would of itself, we think, be a sign of an ill-balanced and imperfect artistic mind.

The true artist's yearning for perfection causes him to feel more pleasure in the perfect representation of a leaf than in the picture of a boundless forest, which, from its very extent, must be imperfect.

And we will venture to say that the poems in " La Légende des Siècles," have, as a group, nothing whatever to do with any Legend of Ages—nothing whatever to do with expounding the enigma of " cette grande figure, lugubre et rayennante, fatale et sacrée, l'Homme " : that they have, as a group, no *idée mère* whatever, save the very familiar one that man's life in the world has been sad and chequered.

An artist's moral system is to be judged not by his direct preachments, but by his artistic representations. If, for instance, he depicts man as acting habitually like a devil, it is idle for him to discourse to us of man as an angel.

Now, a speciality of Hugo's imaginative work,

whether in prose or verse, is that, while he is for ever talking about God and the goodness of God as contrasted with the wickedness of that mysterious and universal malefactor called Society, he so arranges the circumstances of his drama and his stories that the reader is likely to rise from reading them with the impression that there is no God at all, or at least that there is no moral governor of the universe. This must be said not only of the poems in " La Légende des Siècles," but also in such works as " Le Roi s'Amuse," " Notre Dame de Paris," " Marion Delorme," " Lucrèce Borgia," " Ruy Blas," and " Torquemada."

Of course he has a perfect right to represent human life in this way if he honestly believes it to be a true representation.

But the artist who generally divides his characters into two classes—monsters of cruelty and injustice ("les rois " for the most part), and paragons of all the virtues who become the inevitable and helpless victims of these—should not talk about the good God, but should proclaim at once his belief that the world is governed by blind fatality or by blind chance.

The truth is, however, that Hugo has no philosophical system at all, and it is merely because these cruel and violent situations are striking and harrowing that he makes such liberal use of them.

But apart altogether from questions of an ethical or a philosophical kind, it is an artistic mistake to go on heaping woes upon the heads of perfectly innocent people.

The question of the ἁμαρτία μεγάλη spoken of by Artisotle is, of course, too large to be discussed here. And perhaps, if we consider it, Aristotle's requirement was hardly an artistic one at all, for it should be borne in mind that Aristotle required an exhibition of some faults in the suffering hero merely to elude the difficulty of touching upon impiety to the gods, from whose fatal decrees all misfortunes spring.

But, artistically speaking, there is something inherently revolting in such spectacles as the death of Esmeralda, in the drawing of the tooth of Fantine, and in the seizure by the bloodthirsty monks of the Inquisition of a pair of perfectly innocent lovers who are carried off from their dreams of bliss to be burnt alive.

Nor has Hugo that didactic reason for thus shocking us which an ancient writer would have had whose gods were themselves the final cause of the entire tragic mischief—that didactic reason, in short, which Aristotle seems to glance at as being immoral.

Mostly the gods were the direct cause of this tragic mischief ; but as Marmontel has excellently said (*Poétique Françoise*, ii. 119) :—

> " Si, dans la tragédie ancienne, la passion est quelquefois l'instrument ou la cause du malheur, ce malheur ne tombe donc pas sur l'homme passionné, mais sur quelque victime innocente."

These words might almost have been written of Hugo's entire dramatic system ; but then he believes in a God who is not the cause of the tragic mischief, and such representations as those we allude to are as faulty in morals as they are in art. Yet they are striking, and that is enough for most French poets. Reservation of power is now almost unknown in French art.

But we are wandering from the subject of the difficulty poets experience in trying to join flats that have been painted at various times and in various moods. Tennyson affords us a striking example of this in " The Idylls of the King." In 1842 he published the " Morte d'Arthur." For every variety of excellence it was as a " flat " one of the very finest ever produced in this country. He himself, indeed, considered it to consist, as he says, of " Homeric echoes " ; and though this was not wonderful, seeing that all poets consider their heroic poetry to consist of " Homeric echoes," it was wonderful that Landor should pronounce it not only " more Homeric than any poem of our time " (which it could so easily be), but also say it " rivalled some of the noblest parts of the Odyssey " ; for no one knew better than Landor that the " Morte d'Arthur " is Virgilian, or rather it is Virgil plus Lucretius. Years afterwards Tennyson produced a good many flats, exceedingly fine too, exceedingly like each other, and exceedingly unlike flat the first, and again at intervals he produced others equally unlike the richly painted flat with which he began. And then he proceeded to join them. The idyllic simplicity of " Enid " became absolute baldness by the side of the magnificence of the " Morte d'Arthur " ; the magnificence of the " Morte

d'Arthur " became something like magnilo-
quence by the side of " Enid." With " The
Lotos Eaters," however, Tennyson was more
successful in joining the flats produced at
various times. It is one of the finest poems in
the world.

As to " Dieu," if we were to accept Hugo's
conception of Dieu, what kind of a Dieu should
we get ?

And here it may be worth while to discuss a
question which is, we think, very important.
How is it that so few poets could, even granting
them the genius, produce work to affect the
reader as Tennyson's " Rizpah " does ? The
answer is that it is because a story in which is
contained such a vast amount of pity and terror
cannot be treated in any way that is tolerable
at all save by a poet who is entirely superior to
the infirmity common to most poets—pride of
poetic power.

Pride of power has never yet been treated as
an important agent of poetical production. It
may be said, no doubt, that after vanity, which
is first, pride is the great motor of human
action.

Just as a man with an exceptional power of
wind and limb takes pride in risking his neck
on Mont Blanc, and just as a rich citizen takes
pride in displaying the length and strength of
his purse, so the poet, the moment he is hailed
as the possessor of poetical power, feels impelled at once to pose as a poetical athlete.
He knows well enough, of course, that his duty
as an artist is to use pity and terror merely so

as to produce an effect which is at bottom pleasurable. But he cares nothing at all about giving his readers pleasure. He wants to display his power. He must give us pictures of the "Furies" so terrible that he narrowly escapes being torn to pieces by the real furies he has awakened in the breasts of his audience. He must give us pictures of hell that make Christianity itself seem wicked. He must harrow us.

He must, in short, show in the style of "Titus Andronicus," "The Duchess of Malfi," "Manfred," "The Cenci," how strong he is at the expense of all the holiest sanctions of art, till mankind becomes sickened at the display, and is inclined to beg the poets to return to their golden clime, and not turn our clime into a pandemonium of unholy passions, or into shambles of blood and bones.

It follows from the foregoing remarks that a most important thing for a narrative poet to exercise his mind upon is the choice of a story.

In considering whether or not a story is adapted for artistic purposes, the poet has to bear in mind that the first quest of a poet, as a poet, is beauty. Whenever a subject is of such a kind that in treating it the poet, in order to avoid the unlovely, must greatly curb his imagination, it is unfit for poetical treatment. There is no truth in art more obvious than this ; yet there is none which has been more ignored in all poetical literature.

Let us turn to two of the many poems in the English language whose plot is derived from the Italian novelists, Boccaccio, Bandello, Cinthio and others—Keats's " Isabella " and Tennyson's " Lover's Tale," both from Boccaccio.

If the poet will touch upon themes that are too painful (and often the poet is an expresser rather than a man who deeply feels)—if he will, for the sake of strong writing, depict Isabella kissing the mutilated head of the man she loved —he cannot expect that all the poetic power in the world will reconcile to his work the mind which is at once healthy and sorely tried. And it is here that Keats has in some degree fallen short of Boccaccio in instinctive surety of treatment.

In Boccaccio's story are the simple words, " She cut off the head, which she put into a handkerchief," instead of all Keats's elaborate details about the mutilation.

With regard to Tennyson, who in his tremendous poem of " Rizpah " depicts the mother beneath the gibbet picking up the bones of her dead son and treasuring them, and goes through it without one false note, would never have failed where Keats fails in his story of " Isabella." But he does so in his " Lover's Tale."

Boccaccio's story of Gentil de Carisendi's adventure with Niccoluccio Caccianimico's wife has the advantage of being one of the most worn of sensational stories, and therefore deserves Tennyson's selection of it. Signor Gentil de Carisendi, a knight of Bologna, according to Boccaccio's novel, loved a married woman of great beauty, but, unlike certain other of

Boccaccio's heroes, was too honourable to declare his passion. Having, however, heard that she had suddenly died, he visited her tomb in order " to please himself with a kiss." He then perceived that her heart was feebly beating, and by the aid of his servant, who had accompanied him, carried her oft to his house at Bologna. Here, on being restored to consciousness by Gentil's mother, the lady gave birth to a son. The coma which in some cases precedes parturition had been mistaken by her friends for death. Notwithstanding his passion, the knight treated her with the most chivalrous deference. And when Niccoluccio Caccianimico, the lady's husband (who was away), returned, Gentil invited him and some neighbours to a supper, and at the conclusion of the feast— imitating " a pretty Persian custom " he had heard of—introduced to Niccoluccio Caccianimico, as the most precious possession in the house, the lady and her son.

From the time of Tuberville's " Tragical Tales," published in 1587, and the drama of " How to Know a Good Wife from a Bad One," published in 1602, down to the publication of Tennyson's " Lover's Tale," this story has been frequently handled.

On comparing these variations with Boccaccio's original, we perceive that the great and all-important point in the treatment of such a subject by poet or novelist is to take care that, as the heroine is to be used, after her rescue, for romantic and poetic purposes, the memory of the sepulchre shall not soil her beauty, as it

soils the beauty of the Mademoiselle Laurence
of Heine's prose story (another variation, by
the bye), and poison it, as if

> The conscious Parcæ threw
> Upon those roseate lips a Stygian hue.

Even in prose fiction, it may be said that whatever adventures the story-teller may record—
however terrible and dreadful they may be—
there must cling to the hero and heroine of a
love story no memory or forecast of the atmosphere of the charnel-house. But when the love
story is also a poem the charnel-house must
not be even hinted at. The " deep dishonour
of death " is ineviable to all, but, as the present
writer has said elsewhere, " it is insupportable,

> " To taste the fell destroyer's crowning spite
> That blasts the soul with life's most cruel sight,
> Corruption's hand at work in life's transition."

Poetry cannot live apart from beauty—this is
now so recognised a truth as to be a truism ;
and though Death, even as a " cold obstruc-
tion," may, as we so clearly see in " Evelyn
Hope," be rendered beautiful, nothing can make
beautiful to the bereaved soul the corruption of
the tomb, nothing can make it other than what
it is—a dreadful satire upon poetry itself, the
saddest and the grimmest exhibition of man's
fate, which the poet, whose function it is not
to " hurt " (as Joubert puts it), but to soothe
and to bless, should be careful to leave un-
touched.

Tennyson has not curbed his imagination at the point where to curb it was so necessary, but paints the lover kneeling there,

Down in the dreadful dust that once was man,
Dust, as he said, that once was loving hearts.

While Boccaccio rescues his heroine as quickly as possible from the contamination of the charnel-house, merely saying that the lover, " lying down beside her, put his cheek to hers and wept."

Conspicuous as the story of Gentil de Carisendi is for that perfect sweetness of style which sets Boccaccio at the head of all Western story-tellers, it is scarcely adapted for purely poetic treatment. For if the charnel-house is a subject unfit for the poet, how much more so are those dreadful stories of premature interment which from time immemorial have been a terror and a fascination for the human mind ?

No story seems fit for poetical treatment which can call up even by suggestion the intolerable picture of a poor soul waking up to find itself in a scene such as that depicted in Tennyson's poem—waking up as this lady, our imagination tells us, is in peril of doing, amid such ghastly horrors, shut out hopelessly from the aid and sympathy of man, not by any human cruelty, but by some awful conjunction of fate and circumstance investing man for the time being with what is more appalling and more paralysing still—the unconscious cruelty of Nature's blind forces.

A living poet of distinction has fallen into

error of a different kind in selecting another story of Boccaccio's, that of the story of " Girolamo and Salvestra." It is difficult to see what poet could avoid the æsthetic perils surrounding the situation involved in a lover entering the chamber of a married woman, and lying by her side, with her husband asleep on the same bed, and eventually dying there. " A full and conscientious record of the poetic vision " would be inadmissible. Yet a conscientious record can only be avoided by such a false and mawkish pretence of rendering as must have been most galling to the poet.

We must now give undivided attention to pure egoistic or lyric imagination. This, as has been said, is sufficient to vitalize all forms of poetic art save drama, and the Greek epic.

The Hebrew poets have produced a lyric so different in kind from all other lyrics as to stand in a class by itself. As it is equal in importance to the Great Drama of Shakespeare, Æschylus, and Sophocles, we may perhaps be allowed to call it the " Great Lyric." The Great Lyric must be religious—it must, it would seem, be an outpouring of the soul, not towards man, but towards God, like that of the God-intoxicated prophets and psalmists of Scripture. Even the lyric fire of Pindar owes much to the fact that he had a child-like belief in the myths to which so many of his contemporaries had begun to give a languid assent. But there is nothing in Pindar, or indeed elsewhere in Greek poetry like the rapturous song, which we have called the great lyric, where alone we get the perfect example of the Great Style.

But what is the Great Style ? The Great Style is far more easily recognised than defined. To define any kind of style, indeed, we must turn to real life. When we say of an individual in real life that he or she has style, we mean that the individual gives us an impression of unconscious power or unconscious grace, as distinguished from that conscious power or conscious grace that we call manner. It is the same in literature ; style is unconscious power or grace—manner is conscious power or grace. But the Great Style, both in literature and in life, is unconscious power and unconscious grace in one.

And whither must we turn in quest of this, as the natural expresssion of a national temper ? Not to the Celt, we think, as Arnold does. Not, indeed, to those whose languages, complex of syntax and alive with self-conscious inflections, bespeak the scientific knowingness of the Aryan mind—not, certainly, to those who, though producing Æschylus, turned into Aphrodite the great Astarte of the Syrians. We might, perhaps say that there were those in Egypt once who came near to the great ideal. That description of the abode of " Nin-ki-gal," the Queen of

Death, recently deciphered from a tablet in the British Museum, is nearly in the Great Style, yet not quite. Conscious power and conscious grace are Hellenic, of course. That there is a deal of unconsciousness in Homer is true ; but, put his elaborate comparisons by the side of the fiery metaphors of scenes in the Bible, and how artificial he seems. And note that, afterwards, when he who approached nearest to the Great Style wrote Prometheus and the Furies, Orientalism was overflowing Greece, like the waters of the Nile. It is to the Latin races—some of them—that has filtered Hellenic manner ; but whensoever, as in Dante, the Great Style has been caught more than in any other European writer, it comes not from the Hellenic fountain but straight from the Hebrew. What the Latin races lack, the Teutonic races have—unconsciousness ; often unconscious power, but often also unconscious *brutalité*. In discussing epic poetry we have spoken enthusiastically of the Northern Epic, the *Völsunga Saga*, but it must be remembered that sublime as is the Northern mythology, it is often dashed with what can only be called primeval savagery : the coarse grotesque mingles with and often mars its finest effects. Even that great final conflict which we have described in our remarks upon the Northern epic—that conflict between gods and men and the swarming brood of evil on the plain of Wigrid, foretold by the Völuseeress, when from Yötunland they come and storm the very gates of Asgard—even this fine combat ends in the grotesque picture of the Fenrir-wol gulping Odin down like an oyster, and digesting the universe to chaos. But, out of the twenty-three thousand and more verses into which the Bible has been divided, no one can find a vulgar verse ; for the Great Style allows the stylist to touch upon any subject with no risk of defile-ment. This is why style in literature is virtue. Like royalty, the Great Style " can do no wrong."

But then it will be said that the English Bible is a translation from a foreign tongue—a tongue as unlike the English as can well be. Just so, and here comes the most interesting fact in the history of all literature, and one upon which it is absolutely necessary that we should linger over. Taine, amidst a large number of hypothetical generalizations which we must take with caution, sometimes lights upon a deeper thing than has been said by any other critic. Among these deep generalizations we are startled by the following, which explains the vast superiority of the English translation of the Bible over all other translations, and in a certain deep sense makes it an original work. " More than any race in Europe," he says, " they (the British) approach by the simplicity and energy of their conceptions the old Hebraic spirit. Enthusiasm is their natural condition, and their Deity fills them with admiration as their ancient deities inspired them with fury."

Of Teutonic graceless unconsciousness, the Anglo-Saxons have by far the largest endow-ment. They wanted another element, in short, not the Hellenic element ; for there never was a

greater mistake than that of supposing that
Hellenism can be engrafted on Teutonism and
live ; as Landor and Arnold—two of the finest
minds of modern times—have testified by their
failures.

But, long before the memorable Hampton
Court Conference ; long before the Bishop's
Bible or Coverdale's Bible ; long before even
Aldhelm's time—Hebraism had been flowing
over and enriching the Anglo-Saxon mind.
From the time when Cædmon, the forlorn cow-
herd, fell asleep beneath the stars by the stable-
door, and was bidden to sing the Biblical story,
Anglo-Saxon literature grew more and more
Hebraic. Yet, in a certain sense, the Hebraism
in which the English mind was steeped had been
Hebraism at second hand—that of the Vulgate
mainly—till Tyndale's time, or rather till the
present Authorized Version of the Bible appeared
in 1611. " There is no book," says Selden,
" so translated as the Bible for the purpose.
If I translate a French book into English, I
turn it into English phrase, not into French-
English. " Il fait froid," I say, "'tis cold, not
it makes cold ; but the Bible is rather translated into English words than into English
phrase. The Hebraisms are kept, and the
phrase of that language is kept."

And in great measure this is true, no doubt ;
yet literal accuracy—importation of Hebraisms
—was not of itself enough to produce a translation in the Great Style—a translation such as
this, which, as Coleridge says, makes us think
that " the translators themselves were inspired,"

Taine's deep theory is required to explain it. To reproduce the Great Style of the original in a Western idiom, the happiest combination of circumstances was necessary. The temper of the people receiving must, notwithstanding all differences of habitation and civilization, be elementally in harmony with that of the people giving ; that is, it must be poetic rather than ratiocinative. Society must not be too complex—its tone must not be too knowing and self-glorifying. The accepted pyschology of the time must not be the psychology of the scalpel —the metaphysics must not be the metaphysics of newspaper cynicism ; above all, enthusiasm and vulgarity must not be considered synonymous terms ; above all the enthusiasm mentioned by Taine is necessary. That this is the kind of national temper necessary to such a work might have been demonstrated by an argument *a priori*. It was the temper of the English nation when the Bible was translated. That noble heroism—born of faith in God and belief in the high duties of man—which we have lost for the hour—was in the very atmosphere that hung over the island. And style in real life, which now, as a consequence of our loss, does not exist at all among Englishmen, having given place in all classes to manner—flourished then in all its charm. And in literature it was the same ; not even the euphuism imported from the Continent could really destroy or even seriously damage the then national sense of style.

Then, as to the form of literature adopted in

the translation, what must that be ? Evidently
it must be some kind of form which can do all
the high work that is generally left to metrical
language, and yet must be free from any soupçon of that " artifice " in the " abandonment "
of which, says an Arabian historian, " true art
alone lies." For, this is most noteworthy, that
of literature as an art, the Semites show but
small conception, even in Job. It was too
sacred for that—drama and epic in the Aryan
sense were alike unknown.

But if the translation must not be metrical
in the common acceptation of that word,
neither must it be prose ; we will not say logical
prose ; for all prose, however high may be its
flights, however poetic and emotive, must
always be logical underneath, must always be
chained by a logical chain, and earth-bound
like a captive balloon ; just as poetry, on the
other hand, however didactic and even ratiocinative it may become, must always be steeped
in emotion. It must be neither verse nor prose,
it seems. It must be a new movement altogether. The musical movement of the English
Bible is a new movement ; let us call it " Bible
Rhythm." And the movement was devised
thus : Difficulty is the worker of modern miracles.
Thanks to Difficulty—thanks to the conflict
between what Selden calls " Hebrew phrase
and English phrase," the translators fashioned,
or rather, Difficulty fashioned for them, a movement which was neither one nor wholly the
other—a movement which, for naïveté and
pathos in the narrative portions, for music,

variety, splendour and sublimity, in the purely lyrical portions is above all the effects of English poetic art, above all the rhythms and all the rhymes of the modern world—a movement, indeed, which is a form of art of itself—but a form in which " artifice " is really " abandoned " at last.   This rhythm it is that runs through the English Prayer-Book, and which governs every verse of the Bible, its highest reaches perhaps being in the Psalms.   Referring to what has been previously said as to the fundamental difference between structural poetry and prose with regard to expectation of cadence, the great features of Bible Rhythm are a recognised music apart from a recognised law —" Artifice " so completely abandoned that we forget we are in the realm of art—pauses so divinely set that they seem to be " woodnotes wild," though all the while they are, and must be, governed by a mysterious law too subtly sweet to be formulated ; and all kinds of beauties infinitely beyond the triumphs of the metricist, but beauties that are unexpected. There is a metre, to be sure, but it is that of the " moving music which is life " ; it is the living metre of the surging sea within the soul of him who speaks ; it is the free affluence of the emotions and the passions which are passing into the words.   And if this is so in other parts of the Bible, what is it in the Great Lyric, the Psalms, where "the flaming steeds of song," though really kept strongly in hand, seem to run reinless as " the wild horses of the wind ? " And it is this which compels us to place the

English Bible at the top of English Literature. A great savant once characterized the Bible as " a collection of the rude imaginings of Syria," "the worn-out old bottle of Judaism into which the generous new wine of science is being poured." The great savant was angry when he said so. The " new-wine " of science is a generous vintage, undoubtedly, and deserves all the respect it gets from us, so do those who make it and serve it out ; they have so much intelligence ; they are so honest and so fearless. But whatever may become of their wine in a few years, when the wine-dealers shall have passed away, when the savant is forgotten as any star-gazer of Chaldæa—the " old-bottle " is going to be older yet. For that which decides the vitality of any book is precisely that which decides the value of any human soul—not the knowledge it contains, but simply the attitude it assumes towards the universe, unseen as well as seen. The attitude of the Bible is just that which every soul must, in its highest and truest moods always assume—that of a wise wonder and a noble humility in front of such a universe as this. This is why—like Alexander's mirror— like that most precious " Cup of Jemshîd " imagined by the Persians—the Bible reflects to-day, and will reflect for ever, every wave of human emotion, every passing event of human life—reflect them as faithfully as it did to the great and simple people in whose great and simple tongue it was written. Coming from the *Vernunft* of Man, it goes straight to the *Vernunft*. This is the kind of literature that never does die.

The very quintessence of the Bible is the
Book of the Psalms.   Therefore the universal
passion for Psalm-singing is not wonderful ; the
wonder is that, liking so much to sing, they
can find it possible to sing so badly.   It is not
wonderful that the court of Francis I. should
yearn to sing Psalms ; the wonderful thing is
that they should find it in their hearts to sing
Marot's Psalms when they might have sung
David's—that Her Majesty the Queen could
sing to a fashionable jig, " O Lord, rebuke me
not in thine indignation " ; and that Anthony,
King of Navarre, could sing to the air of a
dance of Poitou, " Stand up, O Lord, to revenge
my quarrel."   For, although it is given to the
very frogs, according to Pascal, to find music in
their own croaking, the ears that can find music
in such frogs as Marot in France, in England
such frogs as Brady and Tate, and in Scotland
such frogs as Rous, must be of a peculiar con-
volution.

When Macaulay's tiresome New Zealander
has done contemplating the ruins on London
Bridge, and turned into the deserted British
Museum to study us through our books—what
volume can he take as the representative one—
what book, above all others, can the ghostly
librarian select to give him the truest, the
profoundest insight into the character of the
strange people who had made such a great
figure in the earth ?   We, for our part, should
not hesitate to give him the English Book of
Common Prayer, with the authorised version
of the Psalms at the end, as representing the

modern British mind in its most exalted and its most abject phases. That in the same volume can be found side by side the beauty and pathos of the English Litany, the grandeur of the English Version of the Psalms and the effusions of Brady and Tate—masters of the art of singing, compared with whom Rous is an inspired bard—would be adequate evidence that the Church using it must be a British Church—that British, most British, must be the public tolerating it.

> " By thine Agony and bloody Sweat ; by thy Cross and Passion; by thy precious Death and Burial ; by thy glorious Resurrection, and Ascension ; and by the coming of the Holy Ghost,
> Good Lord, deliver us."

Among Western peoples there is but one that could have uttered in such language this cry, where pathos and sublimity and subtlest music are so mysteriously blended—blended so divinely that the man who can utter it, familiar as it is, without an emotion deep enough to touch close upon the fount of tears must be differently constituted from some of us. Among Western peoples there is, we say, but one that could have done this ; and now listen to this :—

> When we, our wearied limbs to rest,
> Sat down by proud Euphrates' stream,
> We wept, with doleful thoughts opprest,
> And Zion was our mournful theme.

Among all the peoples of the earth there is but one who could have thus degraded the words : " By the rivers of Babylon, there we sat down, yea, we wept when we remembered Zion." For, to achieve such platitude there is necessary an element which can only be called the " Hopkins element," an element which is quite an insular birthright of ours, a characteristic which came over with the " White Horse "—that " dull coarseness of taste " which distinguishes the British mind from all others ; that " ächtbrittische Beschränktheit " which Heine sneers at. The Scottish version is rough, but Brady and Tate's inanities are worse than Rous's roughness.

Such an anomaly as this in one and the same literature, in one and the same little book, is unnatural ; it is monstrous ; whence can it come ? It is, indeed, singular that no one has ever dreamed of taking the story of the English Prayer-Book, with Brady and Tate at the end, and using it as a key to unlock that puzzle of puzzles which has set the Continental critics writing nonsense about the English for generations :—" What is it that makes the enormous difference between English literature—and all other Western literatures—Teutonic no less than Latin or Slavonic ? " The simple truth of the matter is, that the British mind has always been bipartite as now—has always been, as now, half sublime and half homely to very coarseness ; in other words, it has been half inspired by David King of Israel, and half by John Hopkins, Suffolk schoolmaster and archetype of prosaic bards, who, in 1562, took such of the Psalms as Sternhold had left unsullied and doggerellized them. For, as we have said, Hopkins, in many and various incarnations, has been singing unctuously in these islands ever since the introduction of Christianity, and before ; for he is Anglo-Saxon tastelessness, he is Anglo-Saxon deafness to music and blindness to beauty. When St. Augustine landed here with David he found not only Odin, but Hopkins, a heathen at that time in possession of the soil.

There is, therefore, half of a great truth in what Taine says. The English have, besides the Hopkins element, which is indigenous, much of the Hebraic temper, which is indigenous too ; but they have by nature none of the Hebraic style. But, somehow, here is the difference between us and the Continentals that, though style is born of taste—though *le style c'est la race*, and though the Anglo-Saxon started, as we have seen, with Odin and Hopkins alone, yet, just as instinct may be sown and grown by ancestral habit of many years— just as the pointer puppy, for instance, points he knows not why, because his ancestors were taught to point before him—so may the Hebraic style be sown and grown in a foreign soil if the soil be Anglo-Saxon, and if the seed-time last for a thousand years. The result of all this is, that the English, notwithstanding their deficiency of artistic instinct and coarseness of taste, have the Great Style, not only in poetry, sometimes, but in prose sometimes when they write emotively, as we see in the English Prayer Book, in parts of Raleigh's " History of the World," in Jeremy Taylor's sermons, in Hall's

" Contemplations," and other such books of the seventeenth century.

Yet in spite of this there is not, in the whole of modern history, a more suggestive subject than that of the persistent attempts of every Western literature to versify the Psalms in its own idiom, and the uniform failure of these attempts. At the time that Sternhold was " bringing " the Psalms into " fine English meter " for Henry the Eighth and Edward the Sixth, continental rhymers were busy at the same kind of work for their own monarchs— notably Clement Marot for Francis the First. And it has been going on ever since, without a single protest of any importance having been entered against it. This is astonishing, for the Bible, even from the point of view of the literary critic, is a sacred book.

It might perhaps be said indeed that the Great Lyric is purely Hebrew.

But, although we could hardly expect to find it among those whose language, complex of syntax and alive with self-conscious inflexions, bespeaks the scientific knowingness of the Western mind, to call the temper of the Great Lyric broadly " Asiatic " would be rash. It seems to belong as a birthright to those descendants of Shem who, yearning always to look straight into the face of God and live, could (when the Great Lyric was sung) see not much else.

Though two of the artistic elements of the Great Lyric, unconsciousness and power, are no doubt plentiful enough in India, the element of grace is lacking for the most part. The Vedic hymns are both nebulous and unemotional, as compared with Semitic hymns. And as to the Persians, they, it would seem, have the grace always, the power often, but the unconsciousness almost never. This is inevitable if we consider for a moment the chief characteristic of the Persian imagination—an imagination whose wings are not so much "bright with beauty" as heavy with it— heavy as the wings of a golden pheasant— steeped in beauty like the "tiger-moth's deep damasked wings." New beauty of this kind does not go to the making of the Great Lyric.

Then there comes that poetry which, being ethnologically Semitic, might be supposed to exhibit something at least of the Hebrew temper —the Arabian. But, whatever may be said of the oldest Arabic poetry, with its deep sense of fate and pain, it would seem that nothing can be more unlike than the Hebrew temper and the Arabian temper as seen in later poets. It is not with Hebrew, but with Persian poetry that Arabian poetry can be usefully compared. If

the wings of the Persian imagination are heavy
with beauty, those of the later Arabian imagination are bright with beauty—brilliant as an
Eastern butterfly, quick and agile as a dragon-
fly or a humming-bird. To the eye of the
Persian poet the hues of earth are (as Firdausi
says of the garden of Afrasiab) " like the tapestry
of the kings of Ormuz, the air is perfumed with
musk, and the waters of the brooks are the
essence of roses."   And to the later Arabian no
less than to the Persian the earth is beautiful ;
but it is the clear and sparkling beauty of the
earth as she " wakes up to life, greeting the
Sabæan morning " ; we feel the light more than
the colour.

But it is neither the Persian's instinct for
beauty, nor the Arabian's quenchless wit and
exhaustless animal spirits that go to the making
of the Great Lyric ; far from it. In a word, the
Great Lyric, as we have said, cannot be assigned
to the Asiatic temper generally any more than
it can be assigned to the European temper.

In the poetry of Europe, if we cannot say of
Pindar, devout as he is, that he produced the
Great Lyric, what can we say of any other
European poet ? The truth is that, like the
Great Drama, so straight and so warm does it

seem to come from the heart of man in its highest moods that we scarcely feel it to be literature at all.

Passing, however, from this supreme expression of lyrical imagination, we come to the artistic ode. Whatever may have been said to the contrary, enthusiasm is, in the nature of things, the very basis of the ode; for the ode is a mono-drama, the actor in which is the poet himself; and, as Marmontel has well pointed out, if the actor in the mono-drama is not affected by the sentiments he expresses, the ode must be cold and lifeless. But, although the ode is a natural poetic method of the poet considered as prophet—although it is the voice of poetry as a fine frenzy—it must not be supposed that there is anything lawless in its structure. "Pindar," says the Italian critic Gravina, "launches his verses upon the bosom of the sea, he spreads out all his sails; he confronts the tempest and the rocks; the waves arise and are ready to engulf him; already he has disappeared from the spectator's view; when suddenly he springs up in the midst of the waters, and reaches happily the shore."

Now it is this Pindaric discursiveness, this

Pindaric restraint as to the matter, which has led poets to attempt to imitate him by adopting an unrestraint as to form. Although no two odes of Pindar exhibit the same metrical structure (the Æolian and Lydian rhythms being mingled with the Doric in different proportions), yet each ode is in itself obedient, severely obedient, to structural law. This we feel; but what the law is no metricist has perhaps ever yet been able to explain.

It was a strange misconception that led people for centuries to use the word " Pindaric " and irregular as synonymous terms; whereas the very essence of the odes of Pindar (of the few, alas ! which survive to us) is their regularity. There is no more difficult form of poetry than this, and for this reason ; when in any poetical composition the metres are varied, there must, as the present writer has before pointed out, be a reason for such freedom, and that reason is properly subjective—the varying form must embody and express the varying emotions of the singer. But when these metrical variations are governed by no subjective law at all, but by arbitrary rules supposed to be evolved from the practice of Pindar, then that very variety which should aid the poet in expressing his emotion crystallizes it and makes the ode the most frigid of all compositions. Great as Pindar undoubtedly is, it is deeply to be regretted that no other poet survives to represent the triumphal ode of Greece,—the digressions of his subject-matter are so wide, and his volubility is so great.

In modern literature the ode has been ruined by theories and experiments. A poet like La Mothe, for instance, writes execrable odes, and then writes a treatise to prove that all odes should be written on the same model.

There is much confusion of mind prevalent among poets as to what is and what is not an ode. All odes are, no doubt, divisible into two great classes : those which following an arrangement in stanzas, are commonly called regular, and those which, following no such arrangement, are commonly called irregular.

We do not agree with those who assert that irregular metres are of necessity inimical to poetic art. On the contrary, we believe that in modern prosody the arrangement of the rhymes and the length of the lines in any rhymed metrical passage may be determined either by a fixed stanzaic law, or by a law infinitely deeper—by the law which impels the soul, in a state of poetic exultation, to seize hold of every kind of metrical aid, such as rhyme, cæsura, etc., for the purpose of accentuating and marking off each shade of emotion as it arises, regardless of any demands of stanza.

But between the irregularity of makeshift, such as we find it in Cowley and his imitators, and the irregularity of the " fine frenzy " of such a peom, for instance, as Coleridge's *Kubla Khan*, there is a difference in kind. Strange that it is not in an ode at all, but in this unique lyric *Kubla Khan*, descriptive of imaginative landscape, that an English poet has at last conquered the crowning difficulty of writing in irregular metres. Having broken away from all restraints of couplet and stanza—having caused his rhymes and pauses to fall just where and just when the emotion demands that they should fall, scorning the exigencies of make-shift no less than the exigencies of stanza— he has found that every writer of irregular English odes has sought in vain a music as entrancing, as natural, and at the same time as inscrutable as the music of the winds or of the sea.

The prearranged effects of sharp contrasts and antiphonal movements, such as some poets have been able to compass, do not, of course, come under the present definition of irregular metres at all. If a metrical passage does not gain immensely by being written independently of stanzaic law, it loses immensely ; and for this reason, perhaps, that the great charm of the music of all verse, as distinguished from the music of prose, is inevitableness of cadence. In regular metres we enjoy the pleasure of feeling that the rhymes will inevitably fall under a recognized law of couplet or stanza. But if the passage flows independently of these, it must still flow inevitably—it must, in short, show that it is governed by another and a yet deeper force, the inevitableness of emotional expression. The lines must be long or short, the rhymes must be arranged after this or after that interval, not because it is convenient so to arrange them, but because the emotion of the poet inexorably demands these and no other arrangements. When, however, Coleridge came to try his hand at irregular odes such as the odes " To the Departing Year " and " To the Duchess of Devonshire," he certainly did not succeed.

As to Wordsworth's magnificent " Ode on Intimations of Immortality," the sole impeachment of it, but it is a grave one, is that the length of the lines and the arrangement of the rhymes are not always inevitable ; they are, except on rare occasions, governed neither by stanzaic nor by emotional law. For instance, what emotional necessity was there for the following rhyme-arrangement ?

> " My heart is at your festival,
> My head hath its coronal,
> The fulness of your bliss I feel—I feel it all.
> Oh, evil day ! if I were sullen
> While earth herself is adorning,
> This sweet May morning ;
> And the children are culling,
>   on every side,
> In a thousand valleys far and wide,
> Fresh flowers."

Beautiful as is the substance of this entire passage, so far from gaining, it loses by rhyme —loses, not in perspicuity, for Wordsworth like all his contemporaries (except Shelley) is mostly perspicuous, but in that metrical emphasis the quest of which is one of the impulses that leads a poet to write in rhyme. In spite, however, of its metrical defects, this famous ode of Wordsworth's is the finest irregular ode in the language, for, although Coleridge's " Ode to the Departing Year," excels it in Pindaric fire it is below Wordsworth's masterpiece in almost every other quality save rhythm. Among the writers of English irregular odes, next to Wordsworth, stands Dryden. The second stanza of the " Ode for St. Cecilia's day " is a great triumph.

Leaving the irregular and turning to the regular ode, it is natural to divide these into two classes :—(1) those which are really Pindaric in so far as they consist of strophes, antistrophes, and epodes, variously arranged and contrasted ; and (2) those which consist of a regular succession of regular stanzas. Perhaps all Pindaric odes tend to show that this form of art is in English a mistake. It is easy enough to write one stanza and call it a strophe, another in a different movement and call it an antistrophe, a third in a different movement still, and call it an epode. But in modern prosody, disconnected as it is from musical and from terpsichorean science, what are these ? No poet and no critic can say.

What is requisite is that the ear of the reader should catch a great metrical scheme, of which these three varieties of movement are necessary parts,—should catch, in short, that inevitableness of structure upon which we have already ouched. In order to justify a poet in writing a poem in three different kinds of movement governed by no musical and no terpsichorean necessity, a necessity of another kind should make itself apparent ; that is, the metrical wave moving in the strophe should be metrically answered by the counter wave moving in the antistrophe, while the epode—which, as originally conceived by Stesichorus, was merely a standing still after the balanced movements of the strophe and antistrophe—should clearly, in a language like ours, be a blended echo of these two.

A mere metrical contrast such as some poets labour to effect is not a metrical answer. And if the reply to this criticism be that in Pindar himself no such metrical scheme is apparent, that is the strongest possible argument in support of our position. If indeed the metrical scheme of Pindar is not apparent, that is because, having been written for chanting, it was subordinate to the lost musical scheme of the musician. It has been contended and is likely enough, that this musical scheme was simple—as simple, perhaps, as the scheme of a cathedral chant ; but to it, whatever it was, the metrical scheme of the poet was subordinated. It need scarcely be said that the phrase " metrical scheme " is used here not in the narrow sense as indicating the position and movement of strophe and antistrophe by way of simple contrast, but in the deep metrical sense as indicating the value of each of these component parts of the ode, as a counter-wave balancing and explaining the other waves in the harmony of the entire composition.

We touch upon this matter in order to show that the moment odes ceased to be chanted, the words strophe, antistrophe, and epode lost the musical value they had among the Greeks, and pretended to a complex metrical value, which their actual metrical structure does not appear to justify. It does not follow from this that odes should not be so arranged, but it does follow that the poet's arrangement should justify itself by disclosing an entire metrical scheme in place of the musical scheme to which the Greek choral lyric was evidently subordinated. But even if the poet were a sufficiently skilled metricist to compass a scheme embracing a wave, an answering wave, and an echo gathering up the tones of each, i.e., the strophe, the antistrophe, and the epode, the ear of the reader, unaided by the musical emphasis which supported the rhythms of the old choral lyric, is, it should seem, incapable of gathering up and remembering the sounds further than the strophe and the antistrophe, after which it demands not an epode, but a return to the strophe. That is to say, an epode, as alternating in the body of the modern ode, is a mistake ; a single epode at the end of a group of strophes and antistrophes (as in some of the Greek odes) has, of course, a different function altogether.

The great difficulty of the English ode is that of preventing the apparent spontaneity of the impulse from being marred by the apparent artifice of the form ; for, assuredly, no writer subsequent to Coleridge and to Keats would dream of writing an ode on the cold Horatian principles adopted by Warton, and even by Collins, in his beautiful " Ode to Evening."

Of the second kind of regular odes, those consisting of a regular succession of regular stanzas, the so-called odes of Sappho are, of course, so transcendent that no other amatory lyrics can be compared with them. Never before these songs were sung, and never since did the human soul, in the grip of a fiery passion utter a cry like hers ; and, from the executive point of view, in directness, in lucidity, in that high imperious verbal economy which only

Nature herself can teach the artist, she has no equal, and none worthy to take the place of second—not even in Heine, not even in Burns. Turning, however, to modern poetry, there are some magnificent examples of this simple form of ode in English poetry—Spenser's immortal " Epithalamion " leading the way in point of time, and probably also in point of excellence.

Fervour being absolutely essential, we think, to a great English ode, fluidity of metrical movement can never be dispensed with. The more billowy the metrical waves the better suited are they to render the emotions expressed by the ode, as the reader will see by referring to Coleridge's " Ode to France " (the finest ode in the English language, according to Shelley), and giving special attention to the first stanza— to the way in which the first metrical wave, after it had gently fallen at the end of the first quatrain, leaps up again on the double rhymes (which are expressly introduced for this effect), and goes bounding on, billow after billow, to the end of the stanza.

Not that this fine ode is quite free from the great vice of the English ode, rhetoric. If we except Spenser, and, in one instance, Collins, it can hardly be said that any English writer before Shelley and Keats produced odes independent of rhetoric and supported by pure poetry alone. But fervid as are Shelley's "Ode to the West Wind," and Keats's Odes "To a Nightingale" and "On a Grecian Urn," they are entirely free from rhetorical flavour. Notwithstanding that in the "Ode on a Grecian Urn" the first stanza does not match in rhyme arrangement with the others, while the second stanza of the "Ode to a Nightingale" varies from the rest by running on four rhyme-sounds instead of five, vexing the ear at first by disappointed expectation, these two odes are, after Coleridge's "France," the finest regular odes perhaps in the English language.

With regard to the French ode, Malherbe was the first writer who brought it to perfection. Malherbe showed also more variety of mood than it is the fashion just now to credit him with. This may be specially noted in his "Ode to Louis XIII." His disciple Racan is not of much account. There is certainly much vigour in the odes of Rousseau, but it is not till we reach Victor Hugo that we realize what French poetry can achieve in this line; and contemporary poetry can hardly be examined here. We may say, however, that some of Hugo's odes are truly magnificent. As a pure lyrist his place among the greatest poets of the world is very high. Here, though writing in an inferior language, he ranks with the greatest masters of Greece, of England, and of Germany. Had he attempted no other kind of poetry than lyrical his would still have been the first name in French poetry. Whatever is defective in his work arises, as in the case of Euripides from the importation of lyrical force where dramatic force is mainly needed.

VI

THE SONNET

IN poetic art the sonnet—a stanza mostly
iambic in movement, properly decasyllabic or hen-decasyllabic in metre, always
in fourteen lines arranged properly according to some law that is recognised at once as
having universal acceptance—belongs entirely
to the rhymed poetry of the modern world.

Sonnets are divided into regular and irregular.
All regular sonnets are divisible into : (1) The
sonnet of simple stanza in which the staves
follow each other in three quatrains of alternate
rhymes clinched at last by a couplet. This
form is for obvious reasons called the Shakespearean sonnet. (2) The sonnet of compound
stanza divided generally, but not always, both
as regards sense-rhythm and metre-rhythm,
into two parts—an octave consisting of eight
lines (the first line of which rhymes with the
fourth, the fifth, and the eighth lines, the second
line with the third, the sixth, and the seventh),

and a sestet consisting of six lines running on two or else three rhymes in an arrangement which, though free from prescription, must always act as a response by way of either ebb or flow to the metrical billow embodied in the octave. This form is for equally obvious reasons called Petrarchan.

Though poetic art has many functions and many methods, the two following among its functions seem specially to concern us in treating of the sonnet : The function of giving spontaneous voice to the emotions and passions of the poet's soul : and the function of poetising didactic matter and bringing it into poetic art.

With regard to the first of these functions, although the sonnet is a good medium for expressing passion and emotion, it cannot be said to take precedence in this respect of other and less inherently monumental forms. The ode of Sappho, the bird-like song of Catullus, and the free-moving rhymed lyric of modern times are probably better adapted to give expression to simple passion at white heat—while on the other hand they are certainly better adapted to give voice to that less intense form of passion which can pause to deck itself with the flowers of a beautiful fancy—than is the sonnet—

even the sonnet of simple stanza of Shakespeare and Drayton. With regard, however, to
the second of the above-mentioned functions of
the poet—that of poetising didactic matter—a
function which of course can only be exercised
by passing the didactic matter through a
laboratory as creative and as recreative as
nature's own, the laboratory of a true poet's
imagination, the pure lyric must of course
yield to the sonnet. Indeed, it is an open
question whether since the Romantic revival
the sonnet has not been gradually taking precedence of most other forms as an embodiment
of poetised didactics. And should this on
inquiry be found to be the case, the importance
of this form will be made manifest. For as the
mind of man widens in mere knowledge and
intelligence fresh prose material is being furnished for the poetic laboratory every day.
And the question, What is the poetic form best
suited to embody and secure this ever-increasing and ever-varying wealth ?—a question
which has to be answered by each literature,
and indeed by each period of each literature,
for itself—goes to the root of poetic criticism.
Of course, before didactic matter can become
anything more than versified prose, it has to be

excarnated from the prose tissue in which all
such matter takes birth, and then incarnated
anew in the spiritualised tissue of which the
poetic body is and must always be composed.
Hence it is not enough for the poet to use the
sieve, ' as Dante would say, ' in selecting
' noble words.' The best prose writers from
Plato downwards have been in the habit of
doing this. When Waller said :

> Things of deep sense we may in prose unfold,
> But they move more in lofty numbers told.

he meant by ' lofty numbers ' those semi-poetic
' numbers ' of the English couplet in which
poetised didactics were in his time embodied—
as in the time of Shakespeare such poetised
secretions of the mere *intellectus cogitabundus*
were put into the mouths of dramatic characters
after the approved old fashion of the classical
dramatists.

Since the Romantic revival, however, poetic
art has undergone an entire change. Acted
drama cannot now receive poetised didactics,
which would in these days slacken the movement and disturb the illusion required, while
as to the kind of epigram-in-solution or half-
poetised quintessential prose which is embodied

in the 18th-century couplet the criticism of the
Romantic revival is apt to consider this not so
much as poetry as an intermediate form—
and an extremely rich and precious one—
between poetry and prose. Epigrammatic
matter must, to exist at all, be knowing, and as
knowingness and romanticism are mutually
destructive, it is evident that some form other
than the couplet, which is so associated with
epigram, must in our time be used for the
poetising of didactic matter of the unworldly
and lofty kind. And the sonnet of octave and
sestet is a form less epigrammatic than any
other—a form moreover which can never, as
certain other stanzaic forms can do, embody
mere quintessential prose without proclaiming
its poverty, but must always be poetic in its very
texture—a form indeed which will not bear
one line that is not either in essence or in
method poetic or else ' rhetorical ' in Dante's
sense when he defined poetry to be ' a rhetorical
composition set to music.' So absolutely poetic
a form is this that if it should happen that
the diction will not on account of the subject
bear elevation, it has to be at once poetised by
one of those skilful disturbances of the prose
order of the words of which Wordsworth was
so great a master.

The fact of the word sonnet being connected with *suonare*, to play upon an instrument, shows that a knowledge of music, though perhaps not essential, is of great value to a sonnet-writer. Indeed, owing to the consonantal character of our language a knowledge of music is really of more importance to the English than to the Italian sonnet-writer. Although the ' singing words ' essential to a good song for music need not perhaps be greatly sought in the sonnet (save in the special and somewhat rare form mentioned further on), still vowel-composition and that attention to sibilants which Pindar is constantly showing in his odes —that attention which Dionysius of Halicarnassus extolled—and also the softening of consonantal feet by liquids are extremely important in the sonnet, even although it is no longer written to be set to music. After much practice in the art of rhymed poetry when every feasible rhyme leaps into the brain of the poet the moment that a line-ending has suggested itself to his mind—this attention to structural demands becomes instinctive, and is exercised in that half unconscious and rapid evolution of the mental processes which the witty conversationist shows in repartee, and which the pianist exhibits when touching the key-board—supposing, of course, that the poet is a born rhymer. It is, however, a curious and interesting fact that ever since the time of Piers Plowman (when alliterative measures gave way to rhymed measures) English poets have been clearly divisible into two classes—those to whom rhyme is an aid, and those to whom rhyme is more or less a check. And still more curious and interesting is it, that while three of the greatest poets, Shakespeare, Marlowe, and Milton, belong to the one class, Coleridge (who by endowment perhaps stands next to them) belongs to the other. This is why some of the strongest English poets have not been successful in the sonnet, where the rhyme-demands are very great. For some reason or another the rhythmic impulse within them has not been stimulated, but crippled and tortured by the spur of rhyme.

With regard to prescription in the number of the lines and the arrangement of the rhymes of the sonnet, metrical art offers the reader two opposite kinds of pleasure ; the pleasure derived from a sense of prescribed form, as in the sonnet, the ballade, the rispetto, the stornello, etc., and the pleasure derived from a sense of freedom from prescribed form as afforded by those pure lyrics, in which the form is, or at least should be, governed by the emotion. Now every poetical composition should show at once which of these kinds of pleasure is being offered to the reader, and should also satisfy the expectation raised, for he will experience a sense of disappointment on being proffered one kind of poetic pleasure when he has been led, by the stanzaic arrangement or otherwise, to expect another. Nevertheless, a certain few of our great sonnets are irregular, for a great poet can do anything.

With reference to regular sonnets it is self-evident, as regards the sonnet of compound stanza, that there are four different forms into which may fall a metrical structure consisting of an octave of a prescriptive arrangement of rhymes and a sestet consisting of another set of rhymes that are free in arrangement from prescription. And some years ago the present writer exemplified these in ' four sonnets on the sonnet,' one only of which under the name of ' The Sonnet's Voice,' originally printed in the *Athenæum*, was widely circulated in sonnet-anthologies. These varieties of the sonnet of octave and sestet are : (1) The sonnet in which the stronger portion both in rhythm and in substance is embodied in the sestet. (2) The sonnet in which the stronger portion both in rhythm and in substance is embodied in the octave. (3) The sonnet in which the sestet is not separated from the octave, but seems to be merely a portion of the octave's movement rising to a close more or less climacteric. (4) The sonnet in which the sestet seems to be added to the octave's movement, added after its apparent termination in a kind of tailpiece, answering to what in music we call the ' coda.'

With regard to the second of these varieties —the one exemplified in ' The Sonnet's Voice ' —perhaps the ideal form has the octave in double rhymes, and the sestet in single rhymes. But it has to be remembered by the poet that between the effect of Italian rhymes and the effect of English double rhymes there is a great difference. Save in the hands of a sonnet-writer of great practice in the art of vowel-composition, in the art of using singing words, and in the art of softening our consonantal language, by the proper use of liquids and subtle and concealed alliterations, the English rhyme-beat in the double-rhyme octave of this variety is apt to become too heavy for the single-rhyme rhyme-beat in the sestet. By attention to these requirements, however, the rhyme-beat may be so lightened that this variety may become the most brilliant of all.

With regard to the sonnet of simple stanza, it has two special glories : it was the form adopted by Shakespeare, and in it is written Drayton's famous love-sonnet. Hartley Coleridge wrote some fine sonnets in this form ; so did Keats ; but on the whole it has been neglected in recent times. A renewed attention has, however, been lately given to it by critics of the sonnet both in England and America owing to Dr. Gordon Hake's book of nature poems, *The New Day*, where the Shakespearean form of sonnet is used. Here, by a free use of double rhymes the poet gives a lyrical movement to his verse, which, though an occasional feature of Shakespeare's sonnets, is not a characteristic one.

So flexible is the sonnet that every sonnet-writer can and does put into his work the rhythmic movement natural to his own ear. The fact is that, although in a language like the English, it requires no doubt considerable ingenuity to construct a satisfactory sonnet running upon two rhymes in the octave and two or three in the sestet, the sonnet does not really belong to the poetry of ingenuity. Its ingenuity of structure is only a means to an end, the end being that a single wave of emotion, when emotion is either too deeply charged with thought or too much adulterated with fancy to pass spontaneously into the movements of pure lyric, shall be embodied in a single metrical flow and return. Hence the variety of rhythm in the sonnet is infinite.

The movement of Milton, the movement of Wordsworth, the movement of Keats, the movement of Mrs. Browning, the movement of Rossetti, the movement of Swinburne—the reader knows them all. Between a sonnet of Tennyson's and a sonnet of Rossetti's so vast is the difference as regards rhythmic emphasis that it is difficult to realize that the rhyme structure is the same in the one as in the other. And the same remark applies, though not in an equal degree, to Italian sonnets, in regard to Dante, Petrarch, and others.

It is a mistake to suppose that Keats produced more than one supremely fine sonnet of octave and sestet. No doubt the sonnet ' On first looking into Chapman's Homer ' is, if not the finest sonnet in the language, very nearly so, and can only yield to one or two of Wordsworth's or Rossetti's best. This appeared in Keats's first volume : the critics who failed to see from it what a future lay before the poet simply proclaimed their own ineptitude or their own malignity. But in all Keats's other sonnets of the Petrarchan type there are those signs of hasty and incomplete work which compelled Rossetti to characterize them as " first drafts."

The sonnets on the Shakespearean model are some of them better, and the one upon Homer in this latter form is, beyond doubt, very fine.

But to place in the front rank of sonnet-writers a poet who left but one first-rate sonnet seems scarcely right.

In modern Europe the sonnet has always had a peculiar fascination for poets of the first-class—poets, that is, in whom what we have called poetic energy and plastic power are equally combined. It would seem that the very fact that the sonnet is a recognized structure suggestive of mere art—suggestive in some measure, indeed, of what Schiller would call " sport " in art—has drawn some of the most passionate poets in the world to the sonnet as the medium of their sincerest utterances. Without being coldly artificial, like the rondeau, the sestina, the *ballade*, the *villanelle*, &c., the sonnet is yet so artistic in structure, its form is so universally known, recognized, and adopted as being artistic, that the too fervid spontaneity and reality of the poet's emotion may be in a certain degree veiled, and the poet can whisper as from behind a mask, those deepest secrets of the heart which could otherwise only find expression in purely dramatic forms.

That the sonnet was invented, not in Provence, as French critics pretend, but in Italy in the 13th century, is pretty clear, but by whom is still perhaps an open question. Mr. S. Waddington (*Sonnets of Living Writers*) and several other contemporary critics attribute to Fra Guittone the honour of having invented the form. But J. A. Symonds has reminded us that the sonnet beginning *Però ch' amore*, attributed to Pier delle Vigne, secretary of state in the Sicilian court of Frederick, has claims which no student of early Italian poetry can ignore.

As regards English sonnets, whether the Petrarchan and the Shakespearean are really the best of all possible forms we need not inquire. But, inasmuch as they have become so vital and so dominant over other sonnet forms that whenever we begin to read the first verse of an English sonnet we expect to find one or other of these recognised rhyme arrangements, any departure from these two arrangements, even though the result be such a magnificent poem as Shelley's " Ozymandias," disappoints the expectation, baffles the ear, and brings with it that sense of the fragmentary and the inchoate to which we have before alluded. If, however, some writer should arise with sufficient originality of metrical endowment and sufficient poetic power to do what Keats, in a famous experiment of his tried to do and failed— impress the public ear with a new sonnet structure, impress the public ear so powerfully that a new kind of expectance is created the moment the first verse of a sonnet is recited--then there will be three kinds of English sonnets instead of two.

With regard to the Petrarchan sonnet, all critics are perhaps now agreed that, while the form of the octave is invariable, the form of the sestet is absolutely free, save that the emotions should govern the arrangement of the verses.

But as regards the division between octave
and sestet, Mark Pattison says, with great
boldness, but perhaps with truth, that by
blending octave with sestet Milton missed the
very object and end of the Petrarchan scheme.
Another critic, however, Mr. Hall Caine, in his
preface to *Sonnets of Three Centuries*, contends
that by making " octave flow into sestet without break of music or thought," Milton consciously or unconsciously invented a new form
of sonnet ; that is to say, Milton, in his use
of the Petrarchan octave and sestet for the
embodiment of intellectual substance incapable
of that partial disintegration which Petrarch
himself always or mostly sought, invented a
species of sonnet which is English in impetus,
but Italian, or partially Italian, in structure.
Hence this critic, like William Sharp (*Sonnets
of this Century*) divides all English sonnets into
four groups :—(1) sonnets of Shakespearean
structure ; (2) sonnets of octave and sestet of
Miltonic structure ; (3) sonnets of contemporary structure, *i.e.*, all sonnets on the Petrarchan model in which the metrical and intellectual " wave of flow and ebb " (as originally formulated by the present writer in a
sonnet on the sonnet, which has appeared in
most of the recent anthologies) is strictly
observed, and in which, while the rhyme-
arrangement of the octave is invariable, that
of the sestet is free ; (4) sonnets of miscellaneous
structure.

With regard to what is called the contemporary form,—a Petrarchan arrangement with

a sestet divided very sharply from the octave—
the crowning difficulty and the crowning
triumph of the sonnet writer has always been
so to handle the rhythm of the prescribed
structure as to make it seem in each individual
sonnet the inevitable and natural rhythm demanded by the emotion which gives the individual sonnet birth, and this can perhaps
only be acheived when the richness and apparent complexity of the rhyme-arrangement
is balanced by that perfect lucidity and simplicity of syntax which is the special quest of
the " sonnet of flow and ebb."

The wave theory has found acceptance with
most recent students of the sonnet, such as
Rossetti and the late Mark Pattison, J. A.
Symonds, Mr. Hall Caine, and William Sharp.
J. A. Symonds, indeed, seems to hint that the
very name given by the Italians to the two
tercets, the volta or turn, indicates the metrical
meaning of the form. " The striking meta-
phorical symbol," says he, " drawn from the
observation of the swelling and declining wave
can even in some examples be applied to sonnets
on the Shakespearean model ; for, as a wave
may fall gradually or abruptly, so the sonnet
may sink with stately volume or with precipitate
subsidence to its close. Rossetti furnishes in-
comparable examples of the former and more
desirable conclusion ; Sydney Dobell, in *Home
in War Time*, yields an extreme specimen of the
latter."

And now as to the Shakespearean sonnet.
Some very acute critics have spoken as if this

form were merely a lawless succession of three quatrains clinched by a couplet, and as if the number of the quatrains might just as well have been two or four, as the present prescribed number of three. If this were so, it would unquestionably be a serious impeachment of the Shakespearean sonnet, for save in the poetry of ingenuity no metric arrangement is otherwise than bad unless it be the result of a deep metrical necessity.

If the prescriptive arrangement of *three* quatrains clinched by a couplet is not a metrical necessity, if it is not demanded in order to prevent the couplet from losing its power, such an arrangement is idle and worse than idle ; just as, in the case of the Petrarchan sonnet, if it can be shown that the solid unity of the outflowing wave can be maintained as completely upon three rhymes as upon two, then the restriction of the octave to two rhymes is simple pendantry. But he who would test the metrical necessity of the arrangement in the Shakespearean sonnet has only to make the experiment of writing a poem of two quatrains with a couplet, and then another poem of four quatrains with a couplet, in order to see how inevitable is the metrical necessity of the Shakespearean number and arrangement for the achievement of the metrical effort which Shakespeare, Drayton, and others sought. While in the poem of two quatrains the expected couplet has the sharp epigramatical effect of the couplet in ordinary stanzas (such as that of *ottava rima*, and as that of the *Venus and Adonis* stanza), destroying that pensive sweetness which is the characteristic of the Shakespearean sonnet, the poem of four quatrains is just sufficiently long for the expected pleasure of the couplet to be dispersed and wasted.

The quest of the Shakespearean sonnet is not, like that of the sonnet of octave and sestet, senority, and, so to speak, metrical counterpoint, but sweetness ; and the sweetest of all possible arrangements in English versification is a succession of decasyllabic quatrains in alternate rhymes knit together and clinched by a couplet—a couplet coming not so far from the initial verse as to lose its binding power, and yet not so near the initial verse that the ring of epigram disturbs the " linked sweetness long drawn out " of this movement, but sufficiently near to shed its influence over the poem back to the initial verse. A chief part of the pleasure of the Shakespearean sonnet is the expectance of the climacteric rest of the couplet at the end (just as a chief part of the pleasure of the sonnet of octave and sestet is the expectance of the answering ebb of the sestet when the close of the octave has been reached) ; and this expectance is gratified too early if it comes after two quatrains, while, if it comes after a greater number of quatrains than three, it is dispersed and wasted altogether.

The French sonnet has a regular Petrarchan octave with a sestet of three rhymes beginning with a couplet. The Spanish sonnet is also based on the pure Italian type, and is extremely braceful and airy. The same may be said of the

Portuguese sonnet—a form of which the illustrious Camoens has left nearly three hundred
examples.

VII

THE BALLAD AND OTHER FORMS OF VERSE

M. AMPÈRE, in his instructions to the Committee appointed in 1852-53 to search for the remains of ballads in France, told the collectors to look for the following characteristics :

" The use of assonance in place of rhyme, the brusque character of the recital, the textual repetition, as in Homer, of the speeches of the persons, the constant use of certain numbers,—as three and seven,—and the representation of the commonest objects of every-day life as being made of gold and silver."

Among English writers of historical ballads Macaulay stands easily first, although Lockhart's Spanish ballads make a very fine second.

The very first requisite in a ballad, whether historic or romantic, is simplicity of rhyme arrangement as in the old form of "Chevy Chase."

> "The Persy leanèd on his brand
> And saw the Douglas dee;
> He took the dead man by the hand,
> And said wae me for thee."

Extreme simplicity of metre being the first requisite in a ballad, it follows that Tennyson's "The Revenge" and "The Defence of Lucknow" are, with all their excellence, failures.

In the historical ballad the first requisite is "business." Whatever in the smallest degree interferes with this, whether it is the importation of unbusinesslike matter, or the use of unbusinesslike metre, is injurious. Unexpected metrical effects—fundamental irregularites of pause and stanzaic arrangement—are dangerous.

If, for instance, we are waiting for the expected striking down of the hero, we demand that the rhymes and their arrangement shall be aids in our rush towards the catastrophe; and if we are suddenly brought to a halt by finding no answering rhyme where we expected one, and have to ask ourselves when this expected rhyme is to come, our imaginative pleasure is baffled and thwarted to a certain

extent. The otherwise fine ballad, ' The Revenge,' is very seriously injured by forgetful-
ness of this most obvious law. Long lines and
short lines, long stanzas and short stanzas, are
mixed up without the slightest principle at
moments when the reader's imagination has no
time to wait ; and, moreover, some of the lines
are so harsh as to be with difficulty scanned.
It is a pity, for the ballad has every requisite
but this one. Yet it is doubtful whether Tennyson's genius—energetic always, but never brisk
—is suited to the historical ballad. There are
symptoms of a spurring of Pegasus in the lines
of "The Defence of Lucknow"—a rather
exclamatory style, which an ungallant criticism
would call feminine, and which makes us think
that, varied as were his gifts, this kind of work
is hardly in harmony with them.

As to the Romantic Border ballads, if they
are to be taken as a true reflex of the characteristics of the people for whom they were sung,
it was in the north of England that wild passions
akin to those which we associate with Southern
Europe were in former times seen ; in virtue
as in crime the likeness between the two was
very striking.

Two of the foremost poets who flourished late

in the Victorian period—William Morris and Dante Gabriel Rossetti—men known to be richly endowed with humour themselves, had a theory that in high romantic poetry humour had no place, and this in spite of the glaring fact that the greatest poet in all literature, Shakespeare, was also among the greatest humorists of the world, and was constantly introducing humour into poetry. This makes it necessary before treating of the variety of humorous poetry such as parody, mock heroic, comic opera, *vers de société*, etc., to inquire whether humour has any place in high poetry and, if so, what kind of humour.

In the " Paradise of Fruits," the judge who decided upon the stolen flavours of the pine-apple, was ' the taster without a palate." And, in the same way, we may be sure that, among the sixty members of that famous " Court of Humour " held at Heracleum, the man whose function it was to record the jokes for King Philip was the dullest out of sixty dullards.

For, although the desire to be witty and humorous is universal, it seems to be stronger in dull people than in others. The fact is curious, and deserves the attention of the philo-sophical inquirer. In a classification of dullards,

for instance, the highest place must be given to
the middle-class Briton, yet there are more
jokes cracked over a single Bayswater dinner
than were ever cracked over an Attic wine
party—more " funny " things said in the Stock
Exchange in a single day than were said in a
week at the Mermaid, or in Jerrold's gatherings
by Covent Garden. Yet this, which to the
superficial inquirer seems anomalous, is, as we
shall show, perfectly natural. · There are, indeed, no anomalies in Nature ; we have only
to go deep enough to find everything in harmony.

The true inference to be drawn from the facts
is, not that the dull people have really a stronger
yearning to be facetious than the bright ones, but
that they seem to do so by their superior strength
of numbers, and that, as the one touch of nature
that makes the whole world kin is the desire
to be humorous, humour has been supposed to
be the "principium hylarchicum" of the Cosmos.

Humour is as difficult as poetry itself to be
defined. Critics use the loosest language concerning it : they almost always confuse wit and
humour, and speak of humour as though it were
only another name for wit. Not only are the
two temperamental qualities not the same, but
they are the opposites of each other, although

they are sometimes combined in the same writer.

As we have already hinted, the greatest master of poetic humour that has appeared in English literature since Burns is Hood, as seen in "Miss Killmensegg." Burns, however, stands ahead of all English poets as regards humour, and he often reaches a high mark as an absolute humorist.

Dickens does not come within the scope of an article upon poetry. In treating of the comic opera of W. S. Gilbert, we have to draw a distinction between comedy and farce. The very laws of their existence are in conflict with each other—in conflict so much that where one lives the other must die.

Of Comedy, in short, the breath of life is illusion ; of Farce, the breath of life is mock-illusion. Comedy, whether " broad " or " genteel," is a make-believe. She pretends that her mummery is real. Farce, whether " broad " or " genteel," is the very soul of frankness. By a thousand tricks, which she keeps up between herself and her audience, she says, " My acting is all sham, and you know it." Yet we find all the critics—even Charles Lamb himself—talking of Farce as if she were merely

Comedy with a broadened grin—Thalia with her girdle loose and run wild.

Between the two the difference is not one of degree at all—it is one of kind. The fun of Comedy may be just as broad as that of Farce, as in the Dogberry scenes in " Much ado about nothing " ; and Farce can be just as genteel as Comedy herself, even when putting on her genteelest airs in Tottenham Street or Sloane Square.

But here is the fundamental difference between the two: probability of incident, logical sequence of cause and effect, are as necessary to the very existence of Comedy as they are to Tragedy herself, while Farce would stifle in such air. Rather, she would be poisoned by it just as Comedy would be poisoned by what Farce flourishes on—that is to say, in consequence of reasoning—topsy-turvy logic. Born in the fairy country of Topsy-turvy, her logic would be illogical if it were not upside down.

So with coincidence—with improbable accumulation of convenient events. Farce can no more exist without these than Comedy can exist with them.

W. S. Gilbert's comic operas are all farces— farces of the most brilliant kind. *The Mikado,* although it owes much to the superlative music of Sullivan, is, of course, the broadest farce from beginning to end. And the accomplished actors who represented it spared no pains to show the farcical atmosphere.

It is superfluous to give examples of works that everybody knows. But take the song of " the First Lord of the Admiralty." This is the very perfection of farce. It tells how an office boy, whose function was to polish the handle of the front door, becomes by his assiduity in polishing the First Lord of the Admiralty and " the ruler of the Queen's Navee."

We have now to turn to those artificial forms of verse which for a short time had a vogue in England. Of these the rondeau is perhaps the most notable.

The rondeau is a short metrical structure which in its perfect form is divided into three strophes of unequal length, knit together by rapidly recurrent rhymes and a refrain.

The laws of the rondeau have varied at different periods, and even with different poets of the same period—varied so fundamentally that some important critics have found a generic difference between the " rondeau " and the " rondel " or " rondet."

Rondeau, however, is possibly nothing more than the modern spelling of the word *rondel*, as *marteau* is the modern spelling of *martel*, *château* of *châtel*, etc. When the rondeau was called the rondel it was mostly written in fourteen octosyllabic lines of two rhymes as in the rondels of Charles d'Orleans.

In this variability of structure it contrasts with the stability of the Sonnet. The structure under consideration, whether called *rondeau* or *rondel* or *rondet*, may, it seems, consist of any number of lines from eight to thirteen.

But when we find that the kind of triolet used by Froissart is a " rondel " we are compelled to admit that the names given to this form are very elastic.

In Clement Marot's time, however, the laws of the rondeau became more settled, and, according to Voiture, in the 17th century the approved form of the rondeau was a structure of thirteen lines and a refrain.

> Ma foy, c'est fait de moy, car Isabeau
> M'a conjuré de luy faire un Rondeau :
>   Cela me met en une peine extrême.
>   Quoy treize vers, huit en *eau*, cinq en *ème*,
> Je luy ferois aussi-tôt un bateau !

En voilà cinq pourtant en un monceau :
Faisons en huiet, en invoquant Brodeau,
   En puis mettons, par quelque stratagème,
     Ma foy, c'est fait !

Si je pouvois encore de mon cerveau
Tirer cinq vers, l'ouvrage seroit beau ;
   Mais cependant, je suis dedans l'onzieme,
   Et si je croy que je fais le douzième
En voilà treize ajustez au niveau.
     Ma foy, c'est fait !

All forms of the rondeau, or rondel, however, are alike in this that the distinguishing metrical emphasis is achieved by a peculiar use of the refrain. Though we have the English rondels of Occleve and a set of rondeaus in the *Rolliad* (written by Dr. Lawrence, the friend of Burke, according to Mr. Edmund Gosse, who has given us an admirable essay upon exotic forms of verse), even in such comparatively inartistic forms of verse as those introduced by Herrick and Cowley, and other poets and light versifiers of the seventeenth century, the Poetry of Ingenuity, in the shape of pure dilettantism, has never really flourished in this country—never flourished, for example, as it has flourished on the Continent, where, to write a poem in the shape of a wine-glass or a decanter was considered an effort of high poetic genius ; never flourished as it has done in Asia, where *vers de société* (whether Arabic or Persian, Turkish or Hindoostani) must, to be *vers de société* at all, have a repetition of the same rhyme in every alternate line.

Nay, if we had room here to prove our case, we would have almost ventured upon the assertion that the temper of the English Muse is not really favourable to Poetry of Ingenuity in *any* form, unless it coruscates with fancy or is steeped in the many coloured dyes of life— not even to such simple mechanism as that of the imported double-rhymed *ottava rima* of the modern mock-heroic (which, if we are to judge from the fate of " Whistlecraft," the once-famous " Godiva " of Moustrie, " Maimouné," " Sir Launfal," etc., cannot live unless informed by the robust humour of Byron ; not even to such brilliant, though still simple, metrical rope-dancing as that of " Miss Killmansegg," which could not have lived, we think, without the brilliant wit, and often profound humour, of Hood. While in France metrical skill may be (and, far too often, is) the end itself of versification, it is never in this country more (properly) than a means to an end.

It was not till our own day that this form, together with many other forms of artificial verse, had a sudden ephemeral vogue in England. Some of the English rondeaus written during that brief period are as bright and graceful as Voiture's own.

As to rondeaus on the pure French model of a rhymeless refrain, we believe them to be, even in French poetry, always disappointing and bad, and in English poetry intolerable. We can easily understand why so fine a metricist as Swinburne refused in his *Century of Rondels* to write rondeaus with a rhymeless refrain. Swinburne, who in his *Century of Rondels* was the first to make the refrain rhyme with the second line of the first strophe, seemed as though he would bring the form into high poetry.

Although the origin of the refrain in all poetry was no doubt the improvisatore's need of a rest, a time in which to focus his forces and recover breath for future flights, the refrain in all forms where it is used has a distinct metrical value of its own, it knits the structure together, and so intensifies the emotional energy, as we see in the Border ballads, in the " Oriana " of Lord Tennyson, and especially in the " Sister Helen " of Rossetti.

The suggestion of extreme artificiality—of "difficulty overcome"—which is one great fault of the rondeau as a vehicle for deep emotion, does not therefore spring from the use of the refrain, but from the too frequent recurrence of the rhymes in the strophes—for which there is no metrical necessity as in the case of the Petrarchan sonnet. "Difficulty Overcome," though a legitimate source of pleasure in French poetry even of the most serious kind, finds no place in the serious poetry of England.

We have alluded above to the extraordinary passion that sprang up in England during the eighties of last century, vigorously flourished, and then rapidly subsided, for all forms of artificial verse, of which the rondeau was the most important. It came of course from France. The country seemed ringing with rondeaus, ballads, villanelles, triolettes, pantoums and other forms with equally fantastic names, with elaborate repetitions of rhyme.

That it is possible to have too little of such a good thing as rhyme Walt Whitman's poetic achievements have shown; but it is quite clear that in this, as in all other matters, "too much of a good thing" is a sorer sorrow than too little.

Hence the student after studying these forms turned to the *Leaves of Grass*, and in those marvellous pages found, if not so much joy as the Whitmanians can find therein, still a comfort and a solace such as only he can know who has narrowly escaped being rhymed to death. Not that we have a word to say against artificial forms of verse.

In the art of poetry there are and always have been delights of two opposite kinds : the delight of the poetic art which conceals art, and the delight of the poetic art which makes art manifest. There is the delight afforded by him who hides his art in the Iliad, and there is the delight afforded by the chorus of singers in what are called " fixed forms " ; who did not (and for the world *would* not) have their art concealed.

But here is the difference between him of the Iliad and the writer of the ballades, pantoums, vilanelles, etc., that while it is impossible to have too much of the former, it is painfully possible to have a deal too much of the latter. The feasible rhymes in English are not so numerous but that every reader of verse soon has them at his fingers' ends. For a time it is pleasant to see with what tact and ingenuity the ballade-writer will fill in his *bouts rimés*. But this pleasure does not last long. After reading a few score of ballades the curiosity in the writer's manipulations of his rhymes flags. After reading a few hundreds of ballades what was before simply wearisome becomes intolerable, till at last the very sight of a ballade on the page of a magazine was at the time when these poems were fashionable, calculated to give the reader a painful shudder.

The trick which at first seemed interesting gradually appears jejune and worse than worthless ; and the criticism that applies to the ballade applies to the rondeau, the sestina, the triolet, and those other fixed forms for the inspiration of which the English poet is apparently indebted to Walker's rhyming dictionary.

This criticism, however, does not apply, we think, to the sonnet, even in its most rigid Petrarchan form, for reasons which we have discussed elsewhere.

Between the ballades of Lang (charming as they are) and the ballades of Henley and Mr. Austin Dobson (charming as *they* are) the difference is that of substance ; it is never, and can never be, a difference of spontaneous rhythmic movement, as in the sonnet. Nor is this the only reason why it is so easy to have too many of these artificial forms. There is another reason quite as strong : in art *tours de force*, whether the artist's vehicle be marble or colours, or words, have just as much value and just as little as have prodigies in Nature.

Art, undoubtedly, has her sportive side—a fact which seems to be forgotten by those who rail against the muse of " debonair verse "—that jaunty muse who, leaving heroism and imagination to her sisters Calliope and the rest, says to them : " Do ye think that because ye are virtuous there shall be no more cakes and ale ? " It will not be forgotten that no artistic effort can be challenged if it reach its own proper goal. If " debonair verse " did really represent England's contempory poetry, it would be right to say that such a fact was not exhilarating—it would be right to say that " England's heroism and imagination are not to be judged by her verse at that moment."

The craze reached such a pass that it aroused the wrath of the American poet-critic Stedman, who, in the revised edition of *The Victorian Poets*, gave strong utterance to his wrath and indignation at this degradation of the noblest imaginative literature of any race or tongue.

This was to take the matter much too seriously. The seeds of dissolution were apparent in the thing from the first. And now it is interesting to compare these artificial forms with the forms of the new school of 20th century poets, with Mr. John Masefield at their head.

In answer to these strictures we have but to reply, he who expected to find heroism and imagination in such twiddlings of the lyre as ballades, kyrielles, pantoums, sestinas, villanelles, would be a very sanguine critic. Lang's piece is charming, but it would be so no longer if it pretended to be anything more than a " ballade in blue china." It is not given to man to be heroic while dancing in spangles.

Reginald Scot says in his *Discoverie of Witchcraft :* " Irishmen. . . will not sticke to affirme that they can rime either man or beaste to deathe." Without proferring any opinion as to the lethal wizardry of Irishmen, we, for our part, will not "sticke to affirme" that Englishmen (aided and abetted by Scotchmen and Americans) can rhyme a student of poetry to death. If on Parnassus there is a place at all for the muse of " debonair verse " it is far down on the lowest slopes.

Stedman speaks forcibly, and yet with a

fine judicial temper, about the recent degradation of " the noblest imaginative literature of any race or tongue " by poets who, having nothing to say, say it admirably in *bouts rimés*.

Our great English masters have never known anything of the poetry of ingenuity. Sidney and Drummond and others did no doubt try their hands at the sestina and the like, but then even Sidney's place as a poet is a long way from the first.

The metres in which not only Shakespeare, Marlowe, and Milton, but also Coleridge, Keats, and Shelley sang, were simplicity itself compared with these elaborate forms—these forms in which, according to Stedman's notion, the " heroism and imagination " of English poetry have now become stifled. The most elaborate metrical structure ever attempted by England's greatest rhythmist, Coleridge, was perhaps the " Ode to France."

But Stedman seems to forget that, on the other hand, where the motive power of a poem is neither passion, imagination, nor meditation, but fancy or some other kind of sport, the self-conscious art of the poet may, and perhaps should, be brought so prominently forward as to proclaim itself for artifice, and Stedman ought to have remembered Schiller's profound remark that " art is sport."

And now as to *vers de Société*.

If the poet depicts contemporary society, ideality is more essential in this form than in any other department of poetic art. This is what we mean : so perennially fresh is Nature— so infinite in the variety of her beauty—that she may be rendered with the photographic accuracy of Tennyson and the sympathy of Wordsworth and beauty will be the result.

And as to the great elemental characteristics of human nature so eternally interesting are they—so rich in colour are the universal passions of man—that these, too, may be painted with close realism and, again, beauty may be the result.

But, with convention, it is not so. Yet through every poem, no matter what the subject—be it joyful or sad, heroic or terrible— the breath of beauty must be felt blowing like a breeze from Heaven : and *vers de société* are no exception.

But no poet could ever make modern society beautiful ; the painting, even in prose, of London " society " realistically would result in something quite unreadable.

This is why most writers of *vers de société* adopt the cynicism, which, through the mere expression of Thackeray's individual temperament, Robertson and the kettledrum dramatists mistook, it seems, for the temperament of a class.

It follows, therefore, that the writer of *vers de société* must imagine a form of society of his own, or go to societies of the past for his pictures.

The best *vers de société* are rarely the production of those who have seen most—the Buckinghams, the Rochesters, the Dorsets—but of those who have the advantage of that " distance " which (in the case of courts especially) " lends enchantment to the view."

For we do not consider such moralisings as the " Conseils à une Parisienne," and " A la mi-Carême " of that darling of the court, Alfred de Musset, *vers de société* in the proper sense of that word, but satires rather—satires in the mood of Byron's " Waltz " ; while the notion that Praed was really a man of society in the general acceptation of the word is a popular error. Something of it he knew, but not so much as he could have seen, from his social position.

Alfred de Musset, too, in some parts of his

" Sur trois Marches de Marbre Rose " has left his impress. By Théodore de Banville, however, the great modern master of dilettantism, he seems to have been influenced not so much as by those earlier poets who have influenced Théodore de Banville.

Théodore de Banville has lately been playing with (in his " Odes Funambulesque " and " Octidentales "), the triolet, the villanelle, and the Malayan pantoum. The temper of the English Muse is against dilettantism ; so, perhaps, is the genius of the English language. One thing is essential in *vers de société*—perfection of form. And this is seen, we think, in our *vers de société*, which, like all the other varieties of the Poetry of Ingenuity, has, in England, as we have said above, to rely for its vitality upon other qualities than those of delicate workmanship. Prior, until the coming of Mr. Austin Dobson, was our greatest name. But the vitality still left in Prior is owing not to his workmanship, but to his exceedingly fine humour. The same may be said with regard to Praed, who coupled a power of epigram—sometimes true, if sometimes false—with an endowment of humour which, though far below Prior's, was still respectable.

And it is just the same with *all* varieties of the Poetry of Ingenuity—mock-heroic, comic story, court poetry, parody, or what not; the flavour must be as bracing, stinging, and full-bodied as that of British ale.

And if we were asked for a reason for this, we should be sufficiently insular, we think, to say that England is peculiarly the land of " the Poetry of Inspiration "—a complete answer, if true. For the Poetry of Inspiration—that melodious utterance which is born (or is assumed to be born) of irresistible impulse—is the exact antithesis of the Poetry of Ingenuity, that melodious utterance whose quest is " pleasurable surprise " in some shape, such as that of difficulty overcome, or the like. To be conscious and at the same time unconscious, inspired as Cassandra and yet " knowing " as the Jackdaw of Rheims, is altogether beyond the power of any muse whatsoever. In French poetry there is always and properly a pleasurable sense of " difficulty overcome: " hence its delight, among other things, in the barbarism of *rime riche*. But neither in rondeaus nor rondels, villanelles nor pantoums, wine-glass stanzas nor decanter stanzas, can the English Muse give utterance to that " divinity which seizes the soul and guides it at his will." And it is, we think, because English poetry is specially and peculiarly the utterance of that " divine guide " that the taste for the Poetry of Ingenuity is not strong in these islands, that the taste for dilettantism in poetry scarcely exists here at all.

Form is written neither in rhyme nor in blank verse, nor in prose, but belongs entirely to the poetry of arithmetic, and takes rank with those verses written in the shape of lozenges and bottles which were once in vogue on the Continent.

An extreme instance of the danger of writing serious poetry in elaborate verse is exemplified by a modern poet in a poem called " The Dance of Death." The writer of this poem narrowly escaped writing the finest meditative poem of our time—one of the finest, indeed, in the English language. He escapes doing so simply because he is so much too clever a rhymer for a mere poet, and must needs write it in a sestina —that is to say a sestina of sixty lines.

A sestina is a poem written neither in rhyme nor blank verse, but in so-called six-line stanzas, each of which has to take the last word of the stanza preceding it, and twist it about into some new and fantastic meaning, and then to go on twisting every other line in the same way.

Thus if, as in a certain sestina, the first line in the first stanza ends with " paradise," the second line with " heart," the third line with " tears," the fourth line with " fan," the fifth line with " rose," and the sixth line with " fate," the line endings of all the other stanzas must be "paradise," "heart," "tears," " fan," "rose," " fate," only that each stanza has a line arrangement of its own.

Of course it is not, save from the arithmetician's point of view, versification at all ; therefore, many judges consider it to be the supreme work of poetic art in fixed forms, and laments that the sestina has been " comparatively an exotic in French poetry, as in English, until recent years." French poetry we must leave to the French critics, but that the sestina may remain comparatively an exotic in English poetry is what we earnestly hope.

Now in this form " The Dance of Death " is written. And now for the substance of the poem.

Underlying its deep pathos and solemnity there is in " The Dance of Death " a sort of Shakespearean humour which, as far as we know, has hardly been reached by any other poem. Why, then, has it not taken its place in the first rank of our meditative poetry ? Simply because of the poet's appalling cleverness—simply because his poem, being written in one of the most absurdly artificial measures ever invented even in that paradise of the arithmetical bards, Provence, wants, or seems to want (which artistically is the same thing), that salt of sincerity which is the salt of poetic life.

It is difficult to imagine how sophisticated must have become the ear and the taste of a poet who, setting out to discourse of death in the profound mood of him whose moralizings in Elsinore churchyard are for all times and for all lands, could betake himself to his lyre, arithmetical table in hand, and rack his fine calculating powers to find what are the feasible rhymes for a sixty-two-line poem in which all the stanzas shall run on the same rhymes as those of the first stanza !

No doubt the ingenuity required to construct such a metrical framework and to fill it with real intellectual and poetical ore, is so high as to be in itself a kind of genius.

But between artifice, however high, and art

there is a deep gulf fixed. To an unsophisti-
cated ear this reiteration of the rhyme sound,
which to the poets of ingenuity seems the " be-
all and end-all " of the rhymer's art, gives no
pleasure at all, but irritation—irritation because
the fantastic wrestlings with the lyre proper
to the writer of sportive verse, amusing enough
in their proper domain, are felt to be here
grievously out of place.

Though Death may be approached humor-
ously, as in Shirley's magnificent song, he cannot without offence be approached with the
mincing steps of the dancing-master. The
moment that, in the first stanza, the serious
attention of the reader has been arrested upon
the greatest of all subjects, Death's omnipotence,
he naturally expects, even underneath the
poet's humour, grave and solemn " thoughts to
their own music chanted."

Sincerity, in a word, is what he looks for now,
not all this ingenuity of the mere rhyming acrobat.   To say that all the ingenious manipulations
of the fifty-one lines that follow the first stanza
are lost upon the reader is not to say nearly
enough ; they are resented by the only readers
whom it was worth while to please—resented
as an impertinence.

VIII

ETHICAL POETRY

WE have now to turn to a very important branch of the subject, that is, ethical poetry.

Art has her two great fountains of pleasure quite distinct from each other; one the pleasure of mere representation; the other the pleasure of symbol and ethical *motif*. If a poet will give us a beautiful picture of any beautiful fragment of the varied tapestry of life, he delights us. And, from this point of view, George Sand was right when she said that " l'Art n'est qu'une forme "; and Goethe was right when he said that art is representation. If on the other hand, he incarnates beautifully abstract ideas that are beautiful, he delights us. And, from this point of view, Zoroaster was right when he defined poetry to be " apparent pictures of unapparent realities." But, always, the one thing in art is that the artist should do that which he pretends to do. If he pretends to represent, he must sacrifice all or most things to the representation. If he pretends to symbolize, he must sacrifice all or most things to the symbol.

Although there is noble ethical poetry in the

Western world its home is in the East, where the
doctrine of Karma prevails—the greatest doctrine in all ethical systems. Karma is that
inherent force in every action which, by a law
of scientific necessity superior to all other
powers, brings about the good or evil conse-
quences latent in the action's very essence.
Eastern poetry is full of it to the very brim.
From what we have said before in discussing
the Epic and the Great Lyric, it may perhaps be
inferred that the greatest ethical poetry in the
world is Hebraic. This, however, would be a
mistake. The greatest ethical poetry, it would
seem, is either Sufistic or Buddhistic.

Buddhism has existed for something like
twenty-four centuries. In the area of its
prevalence—stretching from Ceylon and Japan
to Siberia and Swedish Lapland—it surpasses
all other creeds, as it surpasses them all in
the number of its followers, comprising as these
do more than a third of the entire human race.
Yet as regards the doctrine of self-abnegation
the fundamental difference between it and all
other systems save sufism has not been clearly
pointed out. And the fact is remarkable if we
remember the considerable amount of attention
that has been given in Europe to Buddhism
since the publication of Eugène Burnouf's
" Introduction to the History of Buddhism " in
1844. Up to that time, owing perhaps to its
having almost died out in India, the cradle
of its birth, the most ignorant notions were
prevalent concerning it, while Brahmanism was
a familiar subject even in popular literature.

It is true, no doubt, as the French Orientalists have pointed out, that it is in the preaching of benevolence that Buddhism is affined to Christianity. But note the difference between these two benevolent systems : Christianity enjoins benevolence because there is a Ruler who (notwithstanding Evil aud its impeachment) is a benevolent, and, at the same time, an omniscient and omnipotent God. Buddhism, like European Paganism, knows no such benevolent God, but it enjoins benevolence none the less—enjoins it, indeed, *because* it knows no benevolent God. The Buddhistic thinker exclaims, " There is none in the skies to love and watch over you, therefore love and watch over one another." And the same may be said of the sufi poets. It is more than a thousand years ago since a certain saintly woman Rabi'a uttered this sublime prayer :—

" Oh God, if I worship Thee in fear of Hell, burn me in Hell ; and if I worship Thee in hope of Paradise, exclude me from Paradise ; but if I worship Thee for Thine own sake, withhold not Thine everlasting beauty."

If we compare these two systems with European Paganism the contrast is very striking.

" We are quite ready," says the human race, under the teaching of Paganism—under the teaching of all systems except the Christian sufistic and the Buddhistic—" to be benevolent, to practise all virtues, to be tender of life, to be pitiful in suffering—to be very good, in short : " que messieurs les dieux commencent."

But sympathizing profoundly as Buddhism

would do with the Greek mind, if it believed
in a God at all, in that apprehension of the
cruel indifference of the gods which runs through
Greek literature, and which Tennyson has so
admirably rendered in the " Lotos-Eaters," the
temper with which Buddhism meets that indifference is the very opposite of the Greek
temper, as expressed not more clearly in the
Titanic impeachments of Æschylus than in the
lofty ethical moods of Epictetus, of Marcus
Aurelius, and of those other stoics who incul-
cate benevolence as a means of self-culture.
For the Buddhistic temper is precisely that
with which Christianity meets the paternal
guardianship of a benevolent God.

The Western mind seems quite unable to
understand the Oriental doctrine of Karma
described above.

The Hindoo doctrine that he who is kind to
the lower animals enjoys in the next world, as
Mann says " bliss without end," is one of the
most favourite subjects always with the Eastern
poets and moralists. The object with these has
been to enunciate an ethical truth, not to use
an ethical truth as an added ornament to a
brilliant piece of writing, as mostly in Western
poetry. The writer of that very remarkable
Pahlavi M.S. (published in 1872 in Bombay, and
London) Arda Viráf, gives us the vision of a
man whose body—all but the right foot—was
being gnawed in hell by a noxious creature
without a name. He was a sluggard who, when
living, would not work, but who had once, with
the right foot, kicked a bundle of grass before

the mouth of a hungry ox at plough. Here we get a perfect ethical lesson taught by a perfect symbol.

Take again Buddhagosha. When he would teach the lesson of the universality of sorrow and death—he simply tells us the story of the weeping girl Kisogátamí, who, on being told by the prophet she has applied to for help that he could make a medicine to restore her child's dead body to life if she could bring him a handful of mustard-seed from a house where no beloved one had died—went from house to house begging what no one could give her ; for, alas ! " few are the living, but the dead are many."

Here, be sure, the concrete form succeeded the abstract idea, and was, indeed, born of it. Not that there is any reason why a poem, or a group of poems, should be the embodiment of an ethical or philosophical idea.

The method of work of the Western poets seems to be the opposite of that of the great Eastern masters of Ethical poetry, whether Buddhistic, or Mohammedan. It seems impossible to them not to imagine a striking situation first, and, having rendered it, look around for some philosophical doctrine of which it may be used as a symbol ; whereas with those whose temperaments impel them to look out upon Nature not for the pictures as they do—not for sensational situations as they do—but for symbols, the ethical *motif* comes first, the picture afterwards. And—what is really inexplicable, is that even when the Western poet does start with the *motif* first—which is very rarely—he seems at once to lose all his imagination—he cannot give it imaginative form at all —but takes the poem right away from human sympathy by bringing in the cold machinery of fancy.

For instance, so great a Western poet as Victor Hugo can find it in his heart to travesty thus the beautiful Eastern symbols of Karma. To be striking is Hugo's first function. He describes in language which for vigour is quite unmatched in French poetry, Sultan Mourad, a monster compared with whom Genghis Khan was tender—a friend, who among other exploits, strangled his eight brothers ; disembowelled a dozen children to find a lost apple ; sawed his uncle into sandwiches between two cedar planks, burnt a hundred Christian convents ; built twenty-thousand prisoners of war into a stone wall, to avenge an uncivil message received from his enemy ; and who, when he comes, after death, to be tried at the bar of God, is pardoned all his cruelties, and enjoys the promised " bliss without end," because once the whim had seized him to drive away the flies that were teasing a dying pig. And there in heaven is the grotesque picture of pig and Dieu having a discussion on the subject, a discussion which ends by the pig and the victims being weighed in a balance, the pig outweighing the human victims.

There are in the Western world a few poets only—and these include poets like Sophocles, Shakespeare, Burns, Tennyson, Browning—who seem to feel the real pathos of human life as a

whole. Many can feel, and more can express
the fire of personal passion ; at least, they can
thrill us intensely with the cries of an individual
soul in its supreme ecstasy of joy or pain.

But only a few among Western poets realise
the unutterable pathos of the tangled web of
human life as a whole ; a few only see clearly
what a pathetic thing it is to live and die,
surrounded by myriads of others who live and
die—" to be here "—as Corporal Trim says,
" to-day and gone to-morrow "—to come we
know not whence, fluttering for a day or two
" in the sunshine and the rain," to leave it and
go we know not whither ; to feel that our
affections, however deep, our loves, however
passionate, are twined around beings whose
passage is more evanescent than " the flight of
the swift bird across the sky "—nay, more
fleeting (as the Talmud says) than " the shadow
along the grass of the bird as it flies "—beings
dearer to us nevertheless than our hearts' blood ;
and dearer still for this, that when they leave
us we know we shall never see them any more
as they are now, and half dread that we may
never see them any more at all.

Along with lyric intensity at its greatest
this feeling is not found, and the reason is
obvious.

All Art is,—if we search deep enough,—an
expression of an egoism stronger and more vital
than common—an egoism too strong to be
content to " die without sign " ; but lyric art is
egoism's very self. " I enjoy—I suffer " ; this,
from Sappho downwards, has been the *motif*

of all the very finest lyric music. The lyrist, it is true, " learns in suffering what he teaches in song "; but he has learned nothing but the poignancy of his own joys and woes,—" Son ceur est un luth suspendu si tôt qu'on le touche il résonne."

Of the pathos of the human drama as a conception the Western poet generally knows nothing save of that one little part.

In order to feel that deep pathetic meaning of human life that we have been speaking of, a poet must have done something more than feel his own joys and woes ; and he must have done something more than sit in his chamber weaving the high fancies of his soul, as the pageantry of life goes by. He must be able to say, as Voltaire said, with pardonable boastfulness—" At least, I have lived." If he has been " cradled into poetry by wrong " he must have learned therefrom something more than the trick of bemoaning it. He must not only have " loved his beautiful lady " ; he must also, like the Knight of Beauvais, have " loved much to listen to the music of beauteous ladies." He must not only have " greatly loved his friend, he must also have had his sweet enemies and.

"Drunk delight of battle with his peers."

Above all, he must have had the rare faculty of enjoying, through sympathy, the perennial freshness of human youth.

Every-day life, which rhymsters call prosaic and flee from, is not prosaic to him, but a

romance ; and his love of man becomes intensified by the very thought of the evanescence
of man's life ; as the preciousness of a vase,
says Pliny, is intensified by the thought of its
fragility.

IX

The Song and the Elegy

A WORD or two must be said here about the song and the elegy. To write a good song requires that simplicity of grammatical structure which is foreign to many natures—that mastery over direct and simple speech which only true passion and feeling can give, and which " coming from the heart goes to the heart." Without going so far as to say that no man is a poet who cannot write a good song, it may certainly be said that no man can write a good song who is not a good poet.

The *motif*—sentimental, patriotic, or passionate—which starts any song should run simply down to the last line. Otherwise, indeed, the composition almost ceases to be a song in the modern sense of the word, and becomes an ode—an ode not only as the word was understood by the Greeks, but as it was understood by Horace, and in still later times by Coleridge, Shelley, and Keats. This oneness of *motif*, which is the fundamental characteristic of the song, goes far, perhaps, to explain the fact that in most songs the really vital portion consists of but one stanza—often the first—from which the remainder of the lyric hangs as a mere fringe. Among the exquisite song-writers of the seventeenth century Shakespeare was one of those who knew when to stop after the *motif* had been fully expressed ; for it must be remembered that the second stanza, which mars the divine song in ' Measure for Measure,' " Take, oh, take those lips away," is not Shakespeare's at all, but Fletcher's. After Shakespeare's time, however, some of the best English songs written until Tennyson rose have been the work of those who are called " minor poets " —that is to say, poets who have made no attempt to " build the lofty rhyme," while often those who have indulged in that risky kind of architecture have only partially succeeded in the humbler efforts of the song-writer. When a large body of the poetic stream is at the command of the writer, the very magnitude of the forces at work perhaps makes it difficult for him to restrain them for the single expression of a single *motif*. But even unity of *motif* is not enough to lend full vitality to a song. Extreme brevity of structure is a primary requisite even where the *motif* has not been departed from. To all forms of literary art Voltaire's maxim applies, that the most effective way to weary the listener is to say all that can be said upon a subject ; but this volubility is destructive of the very existence of the song.

In a word, it is here that is seen more clearly

than in any other department of poetic art the imperious truth of Hesiod's saying that the half is better than the whole ; it is here that literary self-indulgence—always more or less injurious to literary art—is seen to be fatal. This could easily be made manifest, if it were worth while to instance any one of those fine but half-forgotten lyrics of our time, which nothing would have prevented from passing into universal acceptance had not the poet's embarrassment of wealth tempted him into saying everything that could be said upon the subject in hand.

If brevity is the soul of song-writing as of wit, those " short odes " of the Japanese poets, for a knowledge of which English readers are indebted to Mr. Chamberlain, are " twice blessed," blessing him that gives and him that takes. Love as a sentiment rather than Love as a passion inspires most successful song-writers.

In modern times we have, of course, nothing in any way representing those choral dance-songs of the Greeks, which, originating in the primitive Cretan war-dances, became in Pindar's time, a splendid blending of song and ballet. Nor have we anything exactly representing the Greek scolia, those short drinking songs of which Terpander is said to have been the inventor. That these scolia were written, not only by poets, like Alæus, Anacreon, Praxilla,

Simonides, but also by Sappho, and by Pindar shows in what high esteem they were held by the Greeks. These songs seem to have been as brief as the stornelli of the Italian peasant. They were accompanied by the lyre, which was handed from singer to singer as the time for each scolion came round.

With regard to the stornello, many critics seem to confound it with the rispetto, a very different kind of song. The Italian *rispetto* consists of a stanza of inter-rhyming lines ranging from six to ten in number, but often not exceeding eight. The Tuscan and Umbrian *stornello* is much shorter consisting, indeed, of a hemistich, naming some natural object which suggests the motive of the little poem.

The nearest approach to the Italian stornello appears to be not the rispetto, but the Welsh triban.

Perhaps the mere difficulty of rhyming in English and the facility of rhyming in Italian must be taken into account when we inquire why there is nothing in Scotland—of course there could be nothing in England—answering to the nature-poetry of the Italian peasant. Most of the Italian rispetti and stornelli seem to be improvisations; and to improvise in

English is as difficult as to improvise is easy in Italian. Nothing, indeed, is more interesting than the improvisatorial poetry of the Italian peasants, such as the canzone. If the peasantry discover who is the composer of a canzone, they will not sing it. The speciality of Italian peasant poetry is that the symbol which is mostly erotic is of the purest and most tender kind. A peasant girl will improvise a song as impassioned as " Come into the Garden, Maud," and as free from unwholesome taint.

With regard to English songs, the critic cannot but ask—Wherein lies the lost ring and charm of the Elizabethan song-writers ? Since the Jacobean period at least, few have succeeded in the art of writing real songs as distinguished from mere book-lyrics. Between songs to be sung and songs to be read there is in our time a difference as wide as that which exists between plays for the closet and plays for the boards.

Heartiness and melody, the two requisites of a song which can never be dispensed with—can rarely be compassed, it seems, by one and the same individual. In both these qualities the Elizabethan poets stand pre-eminent, though even with them the melody is not so singable as it might be made. Since their time hearti-

ness has, perhaps, been a Scottish, rather than
an English endowment of the song-writer. It
is difficult to imagine an Englishman writing a
song like " Tullochgorum " or a song like
" Maggie Lauder," where the heartiness and
impulse of the poet's mood conquer all im-
pediments of close vowels and rugged consonantal combinations. Of Scottish song-
writers Burns is, of course, the head ; for the
songs of John Skinner, the heartiest song-
writer that has appeared in Great Britain (not
excluding Herrick), are too few in number to
entitle him to be placed beside a poet so prolific
in heartiness and melody as Burns. With
regard to Campbell's heartiness, this is quite a
different quality from the heartiness of Burns
and Skinner, and is in quality English rather
than Scottish, though, no doubt, it is of a fine
and rare strain, especially in " The Battle of the
Baltic." His songs illustrate an infirmity, which
even the Scottish song-writers share with the
English—a defective sense of that true song-
warble, which we get in the stornelli and rispetti
of the Italian peasants. A poet may have
heartiness in plenty, but if he has that love of
consonantal effects which Donne displays, he
will never write a first-rate song. Here, indeed,

is the crowning difficulty of song-writing. An extreme simplicity of structure and of diction must be accompanied by an instinctive apprehension of the melodic capabilities of verbal sounds, and of what Samuel Lover, the Irish song-writer, called " singing " words, which is rare in this country, and seems to belong to the Celtic rather than to the Saxon ear. " The song-writer," says Lover, " must frame his song of open vowels with as few guttural or hissing sounds as possible, and he must be content sometimes to sacrifice grandeur and vigour to the necessity of selecting singing words and not reading words." And he exemplifies the distinction between singing words and reading words by a line from one of Shelley's songs—

" The fresh earth in new leaves drest."

" where nearly every word shuts up the mouth instead of opening it." But closeness of vowel sounds is by no means the only thing to be avoided in song-writing. A phrase may be absolutely unsingable though the vowels be open enough, if it is loaded with consonants. The truth is that in song-writing it is quite as important, in a consonantal language like ours, to attend to the consonants as to the vowels ;

and perhaps the first thing to avoid in writing English songs is the frequent recurrence of the sibilant. But this applies to all the brief and quintessential forms of poetry, such as the sonnet, the elegy, &c.

As to the elegy—a form of poetic art which has more relation to the objects of the external world than the song, but less relation to these than the stornello—its scope seems to be wide indeed, as practised by such various writers as Tyrtæus, Theognis, Catullus, Tibullus, and our own Gray. It may almost be said that perfection of form is more necessary here and in the sonnet than in the song, inasmuch as the artistic pretensions are more pronounced. Hence even such apparent minutiæ as those we have hinted at above must not be neglected here.

We have quoted Dionysius of Halicarnassus in relation to the arrangement of words in poetry. His remarks on sibilants are equally deserving of attention. He goes so far as to say that σ is entirely disagreeable, and when it often recurs, insupportable. The hiss seems to him to be more appropriate to the beast than to man. Hence certain writers, he says, often avoid it, and employ it with regret. Some, he tells us, have composed entire odes without it. But if sibilation is a defect in Greek odes, where the softening effect of the vowel sounds is so potent, it is much more so in English poetry, where the consonants dominate, though it will be only specially noticeable in the brief and quintessential forms such as the song, the sonnet, the elegy. Many poets only attend to their sibilants when these clog the rhythm. To write even the briefest song without a sibilant would be a *tour de force ;* to write a good one would no doubt be next to impossible. It is singular that the only metricist who ever attempted it was John Thelwall, the famous "Citizen John," friend of Lamb and Coleridge, and editor of the famous *Champion* newspaper, where many of Lamb's epigrams appeared. Thelwall gave much attention to metrical questions, and tried his hand at various metres. Though "Citizen John's" saphics might certainly have been better, he had a very remarkable critical insight into the rationale of metrical effects, and his "Song without a sibilant" is extremely neat and ingenious. Of course, however, it would be mere pedantry to exaggerate this objection to sibilants, even in these brief forms of poetry.

THE RENASCENCE OF WONDER
IN ENGLISH POETRY

THE RENASCENCE OF WONDER IN
ENGLISH POETRY

PART I

IN the preceding treatise on poetry first principles have been discussed with but little reference to the historic method of criticism. This essay, on the contrary, will be entirely historical : it will consist of a survey of the revival in England at the end of the eighteenth century, and the beginning of the nineteenth of the romantic temper—that temper without which English poetry can scarcely perhaps hold a place at all when challenged in a court of universal criticism.

Had this great change been a revolution in artistic methods merely, it would still have been the most important change in the history of English literature. But it affected the very soul of poetry. It had two sides ; one side concerned that of poetic methods, and one that of poetic energy. It was partly realistic as seen in Wordsworth's portion of the *Lyrical Ballads*, and partly imaginative as seen in Coleridge's portion of that incongruous but epoch-making book. As the movement substituted for the didactic materialism of the eighteenth century a new temper—or, rather, the revival of an old temper which to all appearance was dead—it has been called the Romantic Revival. The French Revolution is generally credited, by French writers at least, with having been the prime factor in this change. Now, beyond doubt, the French Revolution, the mightiest social convulsion recorded in the history of the world, was accompanied in France by such romantic poetry as that of André Chenier, and was followed, many years afterwards, by the work of writers like Dumas, Victor Hugo, and others, until at last the bastard classicism of the age of Louis XIV. was entirely overthrown.

In Germany, too, the French Revolution stimulated the poetry of Goethe and Schiller, and the prose of Novalis, Tieck, and F. Schlegel. And in England it stimulated, though it did not originate, the romanticism of Scott, Coleridge, Wordsworth, Byron, Shelley, and Keats. But in this, as in so many matters, while other countries have had the credit of taking the lead in the great human march, the English race has really been in the van. Just as Cromwell and Washington preceded, and were perhaps the main cause of Mirabeau and Danton, so Chatterton, Burns, Wordsworth, Coleridge, Shelley, Keats, and Byron preceded, and were the cause of the romantic furore in France which, later on, was decided by the great battle of Hernani. As the storm-wind is the cause, and not the effect of the mighty billows at sea, so the movement in question was the cause, and not the effect of the French Revolution. What was this movement ? It was nothing less than a great revived stirring of the slumbering movement of the soul of man, after a long period of prosaic acceptance in all things, including literature and art.

To this revival the present writer, in the introduction to an imaginative work dealing with this movement, has already for convenience' sake, and in default of a better one, given the name of the Renascence of Wonder. As was said on that occasion, ' The phrase, the Renascence of Wonder, merely indicates that there are two great impulses governing man, and probably not man only, but the entire world of conscious life ; the impulse of acceptance—the impulse to take unchallenged and for granted all the phenomena of the outer world as they are—and the impulse to confront these phenomena with eyes of inquiry and wonder.' In order, however, to explain the phrase fully it is necessary to postpone the discussion of the *Lyrical Ballads* until we have made a rapid sweep over the antecedent methods and the antecedent thought which prepared the way for the book.

It would seem that something works as inevitably and as logically as a physical law in the yearning which societies in a certain stage of development show to get away—as far away as possible—from the condition of the natural man ; to get away from that despised condition not only in material affairs, such as dress, domestic arrangements and economies, but also in the fine arts and in intellectual methods, till, having passed that inevitable stage, each society is liable to suffer (even if it does not in some cases actually suffer) reaction, when nature and art are likely again to take the place of convention and artifice.

Anthropologists have often asked, what was that lever-power lying enfolded in the dark womb of some remote semi-human brain which, by first stirring, lifting, and vitalising other potential and latent faculties, gave birth to man. Would it be rash to assume that this lever-power was a vigorous movement of the faculty of wonder ? But certainly it is not rash to affirm as regards the races of man, that the more intelligent the race the less it is governed by the instinct of acceptance, and the more it is governed by the instinct of wonder—that instinct which leads to the movement of challenge. The alternate action of the two great warring instincts is specially seen in the Japanese. Here the instinct of challenge which results in progress became active up to a certain point and then suddenly became arrested, leaving the instinct of acceptance to have full play, and then everything became crystallised. Ages upon ages of an immense activity of the instinct of challenge were required before the Mongolian savage was developed into the Japanese of the period before the nature-worship of " Shinto " had been assaulted by dogmatic Buddhism. But by that time the instinct of challenge had resulted in such a high state of civilisation that acceptance set in, and there was an end, for the time being, of progress.

There is no room here to say even a few words upon other great revivals in past times, such, for instance, as the Jewish-Arabian renascence of the ninth and tenth centuries, when the interest in philosophical speculation which had previously been arrested, was revived; when the old sciences were revived; and when some modern sciences were born.

There are, of course, different kinds of wonder. Primitive poetry is full of wonder—the naïve and eager wonder of the healthy child. It is this kind of wonder which makes the *Iliad* and the *Odyssey* so delightful. The wonder of primitive poetry passes as the primitive conditions of civilisation pass. And then for the most part it can only be succeeded by a very different kind of wonder—the wonder aroused by a recognition of the mystery of man's life and the mystery of nature's theatre on which the human drama is played—the wonder, in short, of Æschylus and Sophocles. And among the Romans, Virgil, though living under the same kind of Augustan acceptance in which Horace, the typical poet of acceptance, lived, is full of this latter kind of wonder.

Among the English poets who preceded the great Elizabethan epoch there is no need to dwell upon any poet besides Chaucer. He stands at the head of those who are organised

to see more clearly than we can ourselves see
the wonder of the " world at hand." Of the
poets whose wonder is of the simply terrene
kind, those whose eyes are occupied by the
beauty of the earth and the romance of human
life, he is the English king. But it is not the
wonder of Chaucer that is to be specially discussed in the following sentences. It is the
spiritual wonder which in our literature came
afterwards. It is that kind of wonder which
filled the souls of Spenser, of Marlowe, of Shakespeare, of Webster, of Ford, of Cyril Tourneur,
and of the old ballads ; it is that poetical attitude which the human mind assumes when
confronting those unseen powers of the universe
who, if they did not weave the web in which
man finds himself entangled, dominate it. That
this high temper should have passed and given
place to a temper of prosaic acceptance is quite
inexplicable, save by the theory of the action
and reaction of the two great warring impulses
alluded to in the foregoing passage. Perhaps
the difference between the temper of the Elizabethan period and the temper of the Chaucerian
on the one hand, and Augustanism on the other,
will be better understood by a brief reference
to the humour of the respective periods.

There are, of course, in all literatures two kinds of humour—absolute humour and relative humour. The difference between these is as fundamental as that which—as has been already shown in the essay on " Poetry "—exists between absolute vision and relative vision. That a recognition and an enjoyment of incongruity is the basis of both absolute and relative humour is no doubt true enough ; but while in the case of relative humour that which amuses the humorist is the incongruity of some departure from the laws of convention, in the case of absolute humour it is the incongruity of some departure from the normal as fixed by Nature herself. In other words, while relative humour laughs at the breach of the conventional laws of man and the symmetry of the social pyramid of the country and the time—which laws and which symmetry it accepts as final—absolute humour sees the incongruity of these conventional laws and this pyramid with the absolute sanction of Nature's own harmony. It follows that in trying to estimate the value of any age's humour, the first thing to consider is how it stands in regard to absolute humour and how it stands in regard to relative humour. Was there more absolute humour in the age of wonder than in the age of acceptance?

On the whole, the answer must be, we think, in the affirmative. Chaucer's humour was more closely related to absolute humour than any kind of humour in English poetry which followed it until we get to the greatest absolute humorist in English poetry, Burns.

Perhaps the difference between the temper of one period and another of English poetry could be more thoroughly understood if we were to make a brief reference to the humour of the respective periods. For although humour can be expressed as perfectly in prose as in poetry—more perfectly, perhaps—it is an essentially poetical quality, and may be conveniently considered in discussing Chaucer in relation to the Renascence of Wonder.

The singular fact in connection with Chaucer's humour is its modernness. The prologue to the Canterbury Tales might almost have been written yesterday. It is in no way akin to the humour of his contemporaries.

There are, we repeat, in all literatures two kinds of humour—absolute humour and relative humour : the difference between these is as fundamental as that which, (as has just been shown), exists between absolute vision and relative vision. That a recognition and an enjoyment of incongruity is the basis of both kinds of humour is no doubt true enough ; but while in the case of relative humour that which amuses the humorist is the incongruity of some departure from the laws of convention, in the case of absolute humour it is the incongruity of some departure from the normal as fixed by Nature herself. In other words, while relative humour laughs at the breach of the conventional laws of man and the symmetry of the social pyramid of the country and the time —which laws and which symmetry it accepts as final—absolute humour sees the incongruity of this pyramid itself and of the conventional laws which govern it with the deeper sanctions of what is supposed to be Nature's own harmony. It follows that in trying to estimate the quality of any age's humour, the first thing to consider is how it stands in regard to absolute humour, and how it stands in regard to relative humour. It is a singular thing that in Chaucer's humour we get but little of that abandon of mirth which is the characteristic of all the other humour of his own time, and indeed right down to the time of Rabelais. Pantagruelism, it will be observed, becomes almost cosmic at times, inasmuch as it seems to compare the accustomed laws of the universe with some ideal standard of its own, or with that ideal or noumenal or spiritual world behind the cosmic show that sees the incongruity of the laws of nature themselves.

This kind of humour seems to be based on metaphysics, while the humour of Chaucer is so far akin to that of the relative humorist that both are based on experience. The humorist of this last mentioned kind is, like Rabelais, perpetually overwhelmed with the irony of the entire game of human life irrespective of standards, social or even terrene. The temper of this kind of humorist is to laugh the laugh of Anacharsis, the Scythian philosopher, who, when jesters were taken to him, could not be made to smile, but who afterwards, when a monkey was brought to him, broke out into a fit of laughter and said " Now, this is laughable by nature, the other by art." A child can become a relative humorist, or, as we say, caricaturist, by adding a line to the nose of Wellington, or by reversing the nose of the Venus de Medici. The absolute humorist has been so long saying to himself, " What a whimsical idea is the human nose ! " that he smiles the smile of Anarcharsis when he finds the child laughing at the human nose turned upside down. Chaucer had nothing of the humour of the old Greek who, on seeing a donkey eat, died of a sharp and sudden recognition of the humour of the bodily functions.

The period of wonder in English poetry may perhaps be said to have ended with Milton. For Milton, although born only twenty-three years before the first of the great poets of acceptance, Dryden, belongs properly to the period of romantic poetry. He has no relation whatever to the poetry which followed Dryden, and which Dryden received partly from France and partly from certain contemporaries of the great romantic dramatists themselves, headed by Ben Jonson. From the moment when Augustanism, as it is called, really began—in the latter decades of the seventeenth century—the periwig poetry of Dryden and Pope crushed out all the natural singing of the true poets. All the periwig poets became too ' polite ' to be natural.

As acceptance is, of course, the parent of Augustanism or gentility, the most genteel character in the world is a Chinese mandarin, to whom everything is vulgar that contradicts the symmetry of the pyramid of Cathay. It was, notwithstanding certain parts of Virgil's work, the characteristic temper of Rome in the time of Horace, as much as it was the temper of England in the time of Pope, Congreve, and Addison, and of France at that period when the blight of gentility did as much as it could to stifle the splendid genius of Corneille and of Molière. In Greek literature the genteel finds no place, and it is quite proper that its birth should have been among a people so comparatively vulgar as the Romans of the Empire. A Greek Horace would have been as much an impossibility as a Greek Racine or a Greek Pope. When English writers in the eighteenth century tried to touch that old chord of wonder whose vibrations, as we have above suggested, were the first movement in the development of man, it was not in poetry but in prose.

Yet there was no more interesting period of English history than that in which Milton and Dryden lived—the period when the social pyramid of England was assaulted but not overturned, nor even seriously damaged, by the great Rebellion. This Augustan pyramid of ours had all the symmetry which Blackstone so much admired in the English constitution and its laws ; and when, afterwards, the American colonies came to revolt, and set up a pyramid of their own, it was on the Blackstonian model. At the base—patient as the tortoise beneath the elephant in the Indian cosmogony—was the people, born to be the base, and born for nothing else. Resting on this foundation were the middle classes in their various strata, each stratum sharply marked off from the others. Then above these was the strictly genteel class, the patriciate, picturesque and elegant in dress if in nothing else, whose privileges were theirs as a matter of right. Above the patriciate was the earthly source of gentility, the monarch, who would, no doubt, have been the very apex of the sacred structure save that a little—a very little—above him sat God, the suzerain to whom the prayers even of the monarch himself were addressed.

The leaders of the Rebellion had certainly done a daring thing, and an original thing, by striking off the apex of this pyramid, and it might reasonably have been expected that the building itself would collapse and crumble away. But it did nothing of the kind. It was simply a pyramid with the apex cut off—a structure to serve afterwards as a model of the American and French pyramids, both of which, though aspiring to the original structures, are really built on exactly the same scheme of hereditary honour and dishonour as that upon which the pyramids of Nineveh and Babylon were no doubt built. Then came the Restoration : the apex was restored : the structure was again complete ; it was indeed, more solid than ever —stronger than ever.

Subject to the exception of certain great and glorious prose writers of that period, the incongruity which struck the humorist as laughable was incongruity not with the order of nature and the elemental laws of man's mind, but with the order of the Augustan pyramid. It required the genius of a Swift in England, as it required in France the genius of a Molière, to produce anything like the absolute humour which had died out with Rabelais. In Fielding.

width:974px; height:1562px;

to be sure (notably in *Joseph Andrews*), and once in Addison in the fine description of the Tory Squire in *The Freeholder*, we do seem to get it, but in poetry never.

As to the old romantic temper which had inspired Spenser's *Faerie Queene*, Marlowe's *Faustus*, Shakespeare's *Hamlet*, that was dead and gone—seemed dead and gone for ever. In order to realise how the instinct of wonder had been wiped out of English poetry we have only to turn to Dryden's modernisation of Chaucer ; his translations from Virgil, Boccaccio, and others ; and to Pope's translations of the *Iliad* and the *Odyssey*. Let us take first the later and smaller of these two Augustan poets. Instead of the unconscious and unliterary method of rendering the high temper of man in the heroic youth of the world—man confronting and daring the arrows of Fate and Chance—what do we get ? The artificial, high-sounding lines of a writer of worldly verse whom nature, no doubt, intended to be a poet, but whom " Augustanism " impelled to cultivate himself like a Dutch garden in order to become ' polite ' all round.

That Dryden should fail as Pope failed in catching the note of primitive wonder which characterises Homer was to be expected. But it might at least have been supposed that he would succeed better with Virgil ; for Virgil was born only five years before the typical Augustan poet of Rome, Horace. But then it chanced that Virgil was something much more than an Augustan poet. Nothing, indeed, is more remarkable in connection with the chameleon-like character of Virgil's genius than the fact that in the laureate of Cæsarism and the flatterer of Augustus we should get not only the dawn of modern love—love as a pure sentiment—but also that other romantic note of wonder—get, in a word, those beginnings of mysticism and that speculative temper which made him the dominant figure of the Middle Ages. To all these qualities—to all that made Bacon call him the ' chastest poet and royalist that to the memory of man is known '—the coarse, vigorous, materialistic mind of Dryden was as insensitive as was the society in which he moved.

And does he prosper any better with his own countryman, Chaucer, whose splendid poem, *The Knight's Tale* he essayed to modernise with others ? Upon the *Knight's Tale*, based upon Boccaccio's Teseide, Shakespeare and another built one of the great dramas of the modern

world, and so far from depriving it of the charm
of wonder, added to it a deeper wonder still
—the wonder of their own epoch. This superb
poem Dryden undertook to make Augustan.
Again, see how his coarse fingers degraded
Shakespeare's *Troilus and Cressida* when he
took upon himself to make that strange work
" polite." No doubt the littleness of greatness
is the humorous *motif* of the play. No doubt
Shakespeare felt that there is no reason why
the heroic should not be treated for once from
the valet point of view. But how has Dryden
handled the theme ? By adding to the coarseness of Thersites and Pandarus in the play—
coarse enough already—and by simply excising
all the poetry.

But if his treatment of *Troilus and Cressida*
is grotesque, what shall be said of his treatment
of the most romantic of all plays, *The Tempest*,
where, in order to improve the romantic interest of the play, he and D'Avenant give us a
male Miranda who had never seen a woman,
and a female Caliban to match the male monster
of Shakespeare ? The same fate befel him
when he undertook to modernise Boccaccio.
The one quality which saves the cruel story
of *Theodore and Honoria* from disgusting the

truly imaginative reader is the air of wild romance in which it is enveloped. Remove that and it becomes a story of mutilation, blood, and shambles. Dryden does take away that atmosphere from the story and ruins it. Again, take Boccaccio's beautiful story of *Sigismonda and Guiscardo*. It seems impossible to coarsen and brutalise this until we read Dryden's modernisation.

Nothing shows more forcibly the distinctive effect of the new temper of acceptance than the ill-fortune that befel those priceless romantic ballads which in their oral form had been so full of the poetry of wonder in the days of the poetical past. From various European countries—from Germany, from Italy, from France, from Spain, from Roumania—a stream of legendary lore in ballad form had flowed into Great Britain and spread all over the island, not in Scotland and the Border country merely, but in mid and southern England also, where it had only an oral life. But when there came from the Continent the prosaic wave of materialism which killed poetry properly so called, inasmuch as it stifled for a time the great instinct of wonder, it killed, as far as mid and south England are concerned, the romantic ballad also. For

during this arid period the ballad in the southern
counties passed into type. The " stall copy,"
as was pointed out by that fine genius and variously equipped critic, Andrew Lang, destroyed
the South English ballad. For the transcriber
of ballads for the stall was under the influence
of the anti-poetic literature of his time, and
the very beauties of the ballads as they came
from the reciter's mouth seemed to him bar-
barisms, and he substituted for them his notions
of " polite " poetic diction.

With regard to what we have called the
realistic side of the romantic movement as
distinguished from its purely poetical and supernatural side, Nature was for the " Augustan "
temper much too ungenteel to be described
realistically. Yet we must not suppose that
in the eighteenth century Nature turned out
men without imaginations, without the natural
gift of emotional speech, and without the faculty
of gazing honestly in her face. She does not
work in that way. In the time of the mammoth
and the cave-bear she will give birth to a great
artist whose materials may be a flint and a tusk.
In the period before Greece was Greece, among
a handful of Achaians she will give birth to the
greatest poet, or, perhaps we should say the

greatest group of poets the world has ever yet seen. In the time of Elizabeth she will give birth, among the illiterate yeomen of a diminutive country town, to a dramatist with such inconceivable insight and intellectual breadth that his generalisations cover not only the intellectual limbs of his own time but the intellectual limbs of so complex an epoch as that of the twentieth century.

Poetic art had come to consist in clever manipulations of the stock conventional language common to all writers alike—the language of poetry had become so utterly artificial, so entirely removed from the language in which the soul of man would naturally express its emotions, that poetry must die out altogether unless some kind of reaction should set in. Roughly speaking, from the appearance of the last of Milton's poetry to the publication of Parnell's *Nightpiece*, the business of the poet was not to represent Nature, but to decorate her and then work himself up into as much rapture as gentility would allow over the decorations. Not that Parnell got free from the Augustan vices, but partially free he did get at last. Among much that is tawdry and false in his earlier poems, the following lines describing the osier-banded graves

might have been written at the same time
as Wordsworth's *Excursion* so far as truthful
representation of Nature is concerned.

> The grounds which on the right aspire
> In dimness from the view retire ;
> The left presents a place of graves
> Whose wall the silent water laves ;
> That steeple guides thy doubtful sight
> Among the livid gleams of night.
>
>   ＊   ＊   ＊   ＊   ＊   ＊
>
> Those graves, with bending osier bound,
> That nameless heave the crumbled ground,
> Quick to the glancing thought disclose
> Where toil and poverty repose.

Then came Thomson's *Seasons* and showed
that the worst was over. If we consider that
his *Winter* appeared as early as 1726, and *Summer* and *Spring* in 1727 and 1728, and if we
consider the intimate and first-hand knowledge
Thomson shows of Nature in so many of her
moods in the British Islands, it is not difficult
to find his place in English poetry. No doubt
his love of Nature was restricted to Nature in
her gentle and even her homely moods. He
could describe as " horrid " that same Penmaen-
mawr which to the lover of Wales is so fascinating. Still from this time a new life was breathed
into English Poetry. But the new growth was
slow,

Take the case of Gray, for instance. Not even the Chinese mandarin above described was more genteel than Gray. In him we get the very quintessence of the " Augustan " temper. Yet no one who reads his letters can doubt that Nature had endowed him with a true eye for local colour. And although Gray was not strong enough to throw off the conventional diction of his time, he was yet strong enough to speak to us sometimes through the muffler of that diction with a voice that thrills the ears of even those who have listened to the song of Coleridge, Keats, and Shelley. Gray's chief poem, the famous elegy, furnishes a striking proof of the poet's slavery to Augustanism. While reading about " the solemn yew-tree's shade," " the ivy-mantled tower," and the rest of the conventional accessories of such a situation, the reader yearns for such concrete pictures as we get in plenty not only in Wordsworth and those who succeeded him, but even in Parnell and Thomson. Noble as this poem is, it has a fundamental fault—a fault which is great— it lacks individual humanity. Who is the " me " of the poem—this " me " to whom, in company with " Darkness " the homeward plodding ploughman " leaves the world " ? The thoughts are fine ; but is the thinker a moralising ghost among the tombstones, or is he a flesh-trammelled philosopher sitting upon the church-yard wall ? The poem rolls on sonorously, and the reader's imagination yearns for a stanza full of picture and pathetic suggestion of in-dividual life—full of those bewitching qualities, in short, which are the characteristics of all English poetry save that of the era of acceptance the era of gentility—the Augustan era.

At last, however, the poet does strike out a stanza of this kind, and immediately it sheds a warmth and a glow upon all that has gone before—vitalises the whole, in short. Describ-ing the tomb of the hitherto shadowy moraliser, Gray says :

> There scattered oft, the earliest of the year,
>   By hands unseen, are showers of violets found ;
> The redbreast loves to build and warble there,
>   And little footsteps lightly print the ground.

Now at last we see that the moraliser is not a spectre whose bones are marrowless and whose blood is cold, but a man, the homely creature that Homer and Shakespeare loved to paint ; a man with friends to scatter violets over his grave and little children to come and mourn by it ; a man so tender, genial, and good that the very redbreasts loved him. And having written this powerful stanza, full of the true romantic temper, having printed it in two editions, Gray cancelled it, and no doubt the age of acceptance and gentility approved the omission. For what are children and violets and robins warbling round a grave compared with " the muse's flame " and " the ecstasy " of the " living lyre," and such elegant things ?

And again, who had a finer imagination than Collins ? Who possessed more fully than he the imaginative power of seeing a man asleep on a loose hanging rock, and of actualising in a dramatic way the peril of the situation ? But there is something very ungenteel about a mere man, as Augustanism had discovered. A man is a very homely and common creature, and the worker in ' polite letters ' must avoid the homely and the common ; whereas a personification of Danger is literary, Augustan, and ' polite.' Hence, Collins, having first imagined with excessive vividness a man hanging on a loose rock asleep, set to work immediately to turn the man into an abstraction :

> Danger, whose limbs of giant mould
> What mortal eye can fixed behold ?
> Who stalks his round, a hideous form,
> Howling amidst the midnight storm,
> Or throws him on the ridgy steep
> Of some loose hanging rock to sleep.

There is one Greek poet who in virtue of a few fragments of immortal verse is often placed by critics—and, as we think, rightly placed—at the very head of all lyric poets ; we need only refer, we say, to her who in one quality is first among the poets of the world—first, without a second—in that rare verbal economy which is the very accent of passion when at white heat —Sappho. To write of such a poet as Sappho with any approach to adequacy would tax the best efforts of the best poets. This is how an eighteenth century poet, Smollett, speaks of her :—

> When Sappho struck the quiv'ring wire,
> The throbbing breast was all on fire ;
> And when she raised the vocal lay,
> The captive soul was charm'd away !

If Gray and Collins were giants imprisoned in the jar of eighteenth-century convention, they were followed by a ' marvellous boy ' who refused to be so imprisoned. It may be said of Chatterton that he was the Renascence of Wonder incarnate. To him St. Mary Redcliffe Church was as much alive as were the men about whom Pope wrote with such astonishing prosaic brilliance. This is one of the reasons why he bulks so largely among the poets of the Renascence of Wonder. For this renascence was shown not merely in the way in which Man's mysterious destiny was conceived, but also in the way in which the theatre of the human drama was confronted. This theatre became as fresh, as replete with wonder, as the actors themselves. A new seeing was lent to man's eyes. And of this young poet it may almost be said that he saw what science is now affirming—the kinship between man and the lower animal; nay, even the sentience of the vegetable world : further still, he felt that what is called dead matter is—as the very latest science is telling us—in a certain mysterious sense alive, shedding its influence around it.

With regard to his poetical methods, I have on several occasions partially discussed this matter. I have pointed out that all Chatterton's critics seem to miss a peculiar musical movement governing his ear, which often renders it impossible to replace, by any modern word whatsoever, an archaism or pseudo-archaism of his, whether invented by himself or found in Bailey or Speght. Dominated as he generally was by eighteenth century move-ments, Chatterton yet showed at times an originality of ear that is very remarkable. His metrical inventiveness has never been perceived —certainly it has never been touched upon— by any of his critics, from Tyrwhitt downwards. His influence has worked primarily through the great lord of romance, Coleridge himself, who (partly, it may be, from Chatterton's connexion with Bristol) was profoundly impressed both by

the tragic pathos of Chatterton's life and by the
excellence, actual as well as potential, of some
of his works. And when we come to consider
the influence Coleridge himself had upon the
English romantic movement generally, and
especially upon Shelley and Keats, and the
enormous influence these latter have had upon
subsequent poets, it seems impossible to refuse
to Chatterton the place of the protagonist of
the New Romantic school.

As to the romantic spirit, it would be difficult
to name any one of his successors, except
Coleridge himself, in whom the high temper of
romance has shown so intense a life. And, as
to the romantic form, it is matter of familiar
knowledge, that the lyric octo-syllabic movement of which Scott afterwards made such
excellent use in *The Lay of the Last Minstrel*,
was originally borrowed by Scott from Coleridge. Afterwards, when Christabel was published in 1816, Coleridge speaks of the anapæstic dance with which he varies the iambic
lines, as being " founded on a new principle " ;
and he has been much praised, and very justly,
for such effects as this :—

> ' And Christabel saw the lady's eye,
> And nothing else saw she thereby,
> Save the boss of the shield of Sir Leoline tall,
> Which hung in a murky old niche in the wall."

That this " new principle " was known to
Chatterton is seen in the following extract,
which has exactly the Christabel ring—the ring

which Scott only half caught, and which Byron failed really to catch at all : Coleridge alone caught it entirely and splendidly.

> " But when he threwe downe his asenglave,
> Next came in Syr Botelier bold and brave,
> The dethe of manie a Saraceen,
> Theie thought him a devil from Hell's black den,
> Na thinking that anie of Mortalle menne
> Could send so manie to the grave.
> For his life to John Rumsee he render'd his thanks,
> Descended from Godred, the King of the Manks."

With regard to octo-syllabics with anapæstic variations, it may be said no doubt that some of the miracle-plays (such as the *Fall of Man*) are composed in this movement, as is also one of the months in Spenser's *Shepherd's Calendar ;* but the irregularity in these is, like that which is too often seen in the Border Ballads, the irregularity of makeshift, while Chatterton's *Unknown Knight*, like *Christabel*, and like Goethe's *Erl King*, had several variations introduced (as Coleridge says of his own) " in correspondence with some transition in the nature of the imagery or passion." The " new principle," in short, was Chatterton's.

Again, in the mysterious suggestiveness of remote geographical names, a suggestiveness quite other than the pomp and sonority which Marlowe and Milton so loved—the world-involving echoes of *Kubla Khan* seem to have been caught from such lines as these in Chatterton's African eclogue *Narva and Mored*—

" From Lorbar's cave to where the nations end, . .
Explores the palaces on Lira's coast,
Where howls the war-song of the Chieftain's ghost, . .
Like the loud echoes on Toddida's sea,
The warrior's circle, the mysterious tree."

And turning to the question of Chatterton's
influence upon Keats, it is not only indirectly
through Coleridge that the rich mind of Keats
shows signs of having drunk at Chatterton's
fountain of romance : there is a side of Chatterton which Keats knew, and which Coleridge
did not.

It is difficult to express in words wherein lies
the entirely spiritual kinship between Chatterton's *Ballad of Charity* and Keats's *Eve of
St. Agnes*, yet most critics, I think, will recognise that kinship.   Not only are the beggar
and the thunderstorm depicted with the sen-
suous sympathy and melodious insistence which
is the characteristic charm of the *Eve of St.
Agnes*, but the movement of the lines is often
the same.   Take, for instance, the description
of Keats's bedesman, " meagre, barefoot, wan,"
which is, in point of metrical movement, identical with Chatterton's description of the arms-
craver, " withered forwynd, dead."   More obvious perhaps, yet not more essentially true,
is the likeness between the famous passage in
Keats's *Isabella*, beginning,

" For then the Ceylon diver held his breath,
And went all naked to the hungry shark," etc.

and these four lines in Chatterton's *Narva and
Mored*,

" Where the pale children of the feeble sun
In search of gold through every climate run
From burning heat to freezing torments go,
And live in all vicissitudes of woe."

It was perfectly fit, therefore, that Keats should dedicate his *Endymion* to the memory of Thomas Chatterton. Not that Keats or Coleridge stole from Chatterton : no two poets had less need to steal from anyone. But the whole history of poetry shows that poetic methods are a growth as well as an inspiration.

So steeped indeed was Chatterton in romance, that, except in the case of the *African Eclogues*, his imagination seems to be never really alive save when in the dramatic masquerade of the monk of Bristol.

Then came Cowper, whose later poetry, when it is contrasted with the jargon of Hayley, seems to belong to another world. But it is possible, perhaps, to credit Cowper with too much in this matter.

He was followed by a poet who did as much for the romantic movement as even the " marvellous boy " himself could do. Although Burns like so many other fine poets has left behind him some poor stuff, it would be as difficult to exaggerate his intellectual strength as to overestimate his genius. The dialect of the Scottish peasantry had already been admirably worked in by certain of his predecessors, but it was left to Burns to bring it into high poetry.

In mere style he is, when writing in Scots, to be ranked with the great masters. No one realised more fully than he the power of verbal parsimony in poetry. As a quarter of an ounce of bullet in its power of striking home is to an ounce of duck-shot, so is a line of Burns to a line of any other poet save two, both of whom are extremely unlike him in other respects and extremely unlike each other. To conciseness he made everything yield as completely as did Villon in the *Ballade des Dames du Temps Jadis*, and in *Les Regrets de la Belle Heaulmière*, and as completely as did Dante in the most concise of his lines. As surely as Dante's condensation is born of an intensity of imaginative vision, so surely is Burns's condensation born of an intensity of passion. Since Drayton wrote his sonnet beginning :

" Since ther's no helpe, come let us kiss and part ! "

there had been nothing in the shape of passionate English poetry in rhyme that could come near Burns's lines :

> Had we never loved sae kindly,
> Had we never loved sae blindly,
> Never met or never parted,
> We had ne'er been broken-hearted.

But, splendid as is his passionate poetry, it is specially as an absolute humorist that he towers above all the poets of the eighteenth century. Undoubtedly, to get away on all occasions from the shadow of the great social pyramid was not to be expected of a poet at the time, and in the conditions in which Burns was born. Yet it is astonishing how this Scottish yeoman did get away from it at times, as in " A Man's a Man for a' that.' It is astonishing to realise how he was able to show a feeling for absolute humour such as in the eighteenth century had only been shown by prose writers—prose writers of the first rank—like Swift and Sterne. Indeed, if we did not remember that he followed the creator of Uncle Toby, he would take, if that were possible, a still higher place than he now does as an absolute humorist. Not even Uncle Toby's apostrophe to the fly is finer than Burns's lines to a mouse on turning her up with a plough. But his lines to a mountain daisy, which he had turned down with the plough, are full of a deeper humour still—a humorous sympathy with the vegetable no less than with the animal kingdom. There is nothing in all poetry which touches it. Much admiration has been given, and rightly given to Dorothy Wordsworth's beautiful prose words in her diary about the daffodil, as showing how a nature-lover without the ' accomplishment of verse ' can make us conscious of the consciousness of a wild-flower. But they were written after Burns, and though they have some of Burns's playfulness, they cannot be said to show his humour.

It is in poems of another class, however—in such poems as the ' Address to the De'il '— that we get his greatest triumph as an absolute humorist, for there we get the " cosmic humour " before alluded to—the very crown and flower of all humour. And take " Holy Willie's Prayer," where, biting as is the satire, the poet's humorous enjoyment of it carries it into the rarest poetry. In ' Tam o' Shanter ' we get the finest mixture of humour and wisdom, the finest instance of Teutonic grotesque, to be found in all English poetry. In ' The Jolly Beggars,' Burns now and again shows that he could pass into the mood of true Pantagruelism —a mood which is of all moods the rarest and the finest—a mood which requires in the humorist such a blessed mixture of the juices as nature cannot often in a climate like ours achieve.

A true child of the Renascence of Wonder who followed Burns, William Blake, though he was entirely without humour, and showed not much power of giving realistic pictures of nature, had a finer sense of the supernatural than any of his predecessors.

PART II

A ND now, at last, after this swift and wide circuit, we are able to turn to the central idea of this essay, the modern Renascence of Wonder, which followed the long epoch of acceptance known as "English Augustanism." It is not our purpose in this work to discuss the poetry of any one of the poets of this great epoch except in regard to the Renascence of Wonder. In 1765 Percy had published his famous collection of old ballads, and this directed general attention to our ballad literature. The first poet among the great group who fell under the influence of the old ballads was probably Scott, who in 1802 brought out the first two volumes of his priceless *Border Minstrelsy*. The old ballads were, of course, very unequal in quality, but among them were ' Clerk Saunders,' ' The Wife of Usher's Well,' ' The Young Tamlane,' and the great ballad which Scott afterwards named ' The Demon Lover,' with certain others which compel us to set the ' Border

Ballads,' as they are called, at the very top of the real poetry of the modern world. Coleridge, as we are going to see, could give us the weird and the beautiful combined, but he could not blend with these qualities such dramatic humanity and intense pathos as are expressed in certain stanzas in "The Wife of Usher's Well," and in such writing as this from 'Clerk Saunders,' where Saunders's mistress, after he had been assassinated by her brothers throws herself upon his grave and exclaims :—

> Is there ony roome at your head, Saunders ?
> Is there ony roome at your feet ?
> Or ony roome at your side, Saunders,
> Where fain, fain, I wad sleep ?

Scott, we say, is entitled to be placed at the head of those who are generally accredited with originating the Renascence of Wonder at the end of the eighteenth century.

But great as was the influence of Scott in this matter, it is hard to see how the effect of his romantic work would have been so potent as it now is without the influence of Coleridge. Scott's friend Stoddart, having heard Coleridge recite the first part of *Christabel* while still in manuscript, and having a memory that retained everything, repeated the poem to Scott. The seed fell upon a soil of magical fertility. Scott at once sat down and produced *The Lay of the Last Minstrel*. There is no need to say with Leigh Hunt that Scott's vigorous poem is a coarse travesty of *Christabel* in order to admit that, full as it is of splendid imaginative qualities, it is defective in technique, and often cheap in diction. Some of Scott's romantic ballads and snatches of verse, however, scattered through his novels show that it was a languid artistic conscience alone that prevented him from taking a much higher place as a poet than he now takes. If he never learnt, as Coleridge knew by instinct, the truth so admirably expressed in Joubert's saying that ' it is better to be exquisite than to be ample,' it really seems to have been because he did not think it worth while to learn to be exquisite. For the distinctive quality of Scott is that he seems to be greater than his work—as much greater, indeed, as a spreading oak seems greater than the leaves it sheds. Coleridge's *Christabel, The Ancient Mariner*, and *Kubla Khan* are, as regards the romantic spirit, above—and far above—any work of any other English poet. Instances innumerable might be adduced showing how his very nature was steeped in the fountain from which the old balladists themselves drew, but in a survey so brief as this there is room to give only one. In the ' Conclusion ' of the first part of *Christabel* he recapitulates and summarises, in lines that are at once matchless as poetry and matchless in succinctness of statement, the entire story of the bewitched maiden and her terrible foe which had gone before :

> A star hath set, a star hath risen,
> O Geraldine ! since arms of thine
> Have been the lovely lady's prison.
> O Geraldine ! one hour was thine—
> Thou'st had thy will !   By tairn and rill,
> The night-birds all that hour were still.
> But now they are jubilant anew,
> From cliff and tower, tu-whoo ! tu-whoo !
> Tu-whoo ! tu-whoo ! from wood and fell !

Here we get that feeling of the inextricable web in which the human drama and external nature are woven which is the very soul of poetic wonder. So great is the maleficent power of the beautiful witch that a spell is thrown over all Nature. For an hour the very woods and fells remain in a shuddering state of sympathetic consciousness of her—

> The night-birds all that hour were still.

When the spell is passed Nature awakes as from a hideous nightmare, and ' the night-birds ' are jubilant anew. This is the very highest reach of poetic wonder—finer, if that be possible, than the night-storm during the murder of Duncan. And note the artistic method by which Coleridge gives us this amazing and overwhelming picture of the oneness of all Nature. However the rhymes may follow each other, it is always easy for the critic, by studying the intellectual and emotional movement of the sequence, to see which rhyme-word first came to the poet's mind, and suggested the rhyme-words to follow or precede it. It is the witch's maleficent willpower which here dominates the poet's mind as he writes. Therefore we know that he first wrote—

Thou'st had thy will.

In finding a rhyme-word for ' will ' and ' rill,' the word ' still ' would of course present itself, among others, to any poet's mind ; but it required a poet steeped in the true poetic wonder of '' pre-Augustanism,'' it required Coleridge, whose genius was that very Lady of the Lake,

Sole-sitting by the shores of Old Romance —

to feel the most tremendous and awe-inspiring
picture, perhaps, in all poetry called up to his
imagination—

The night-birds all that hour were still.

The nearer in temper any other line approaches
this, the nearer does it approach the ideal of
poetic wonder. It is, however, owing to the very
rarity of Coleridge's genius that not he but
Scott popularised the romantic movement. In
such purely poetical work as the first part of
Christabel, which was entirely unlocalised, realistic mediæval pictures were not requisite as
they were in the *Lay of the Last Minstrel*. After
such work as Coleridge's all that the romantic
revival needed was a poet who would supply
it with feet in addition to wings. Scott supplied
those feet. However, in the second part of
Christabel, written later—in which the poem is
localised after Scott's manner—Coleridge showed
so much of Scott's influence that it may not be
too fanciful to call these two immortal poets
the binary star of romanticism revolving around
one common poetic centre. Scott's poetry
became so immensely popular that it soon set
every poet and every versifier, from Byron
downwards, writing romantic stories in octo-

syllabic couplets, with the old anapæstic lilt of romantic poetry.

As regards Wordsworth's share in this movement, though it was, no doubt, confined largely to poetic methods, the following superb lines from ' Yew Trees ' can be set beside even Coleridge's masterpieces as regards the romantic side of the Renascence of Wonder :

> Beneath whose sable roof
> Of boughs, as if for festal purpose, decked
> With unrejoicing berries—ghostly shapes
> May meet at noontide, Fear and trembling Hope,
> Silence and Foresight, Death the Skeleton
> And Time the Shadow—there to celebrate,
> As in a natural temple scattered o'er
> With altars undisturbed of mossy stone,
> United worship, or in mute repose
> To lie, and listen to the mountain flood
> Murmuring from Glaramara's inmost caves.

Whether the reaction would have died out (as did the revival of natural language by Theocritus after such comparatively feeble followers as Bion and Moschus) had not Wordsworth's indomitable will and masterful simplicity of character stood up and saved it, or whether, on the contrary, the movement was injured and delayed by this obstinacy and simplicity of character—which led him into exaggerated theories, exposing it to ridicule—is perhaps a debatable question. However, it ended by the "poetic" temper, the "poetic" diction, and the "poetic" methods, of the eighteenth century being swept away. But as to real knowledge of the mere physiognomy of mediævalism, Coleridge and Scott were perhaps on a par. Indeed, imperfect knowledge of this physiognomy was a weak point in the entire group of poets who set to work to revive it. Coleridge showed a certain knowledge of it, which, like Scott's, was no doubt above that of Horace Walpole and Mrs. Radcliffe. But since the great accumulation of learning upon this subject which came afterwards for the use of English poets it seems slight enough. Abbotsford alone is enough to show that Scott did not fully escape the bastard mediævalism of the eightteenth century. But we can forgive Scott all in the matter of exactitude. If he in *Ivanhoe* vanquished every difficulty, and wrote an immortal mediæval romance with not many touches of true mediævalism, that is only another proof of his vitalising imagination and genius. Fortunately, however, Scott was something more than a man like his successor, Meinhold, who had every mediæval detail at his command. Had the author of *Ivanhoe* been as truly mediæval as the author of *Sidonia*, he would have appealed to a leisured few by whom the past is more beloved than the present ; but he would not have given the English-speaking race those superb works of his which are

"A largess universal like the sun."

Though the Ettrick shepherd, in *The Queen's Wake*, shows plenty of the true feeling for the supernatural side of the movement, he had not even in *Bonnie Kilmanny* sufficient governance over his vivid imagination to express himself with that concentrated energy which is one of the first requisites of all poetry.

As to Wordsworth as a nature-poet, there are, of course, three attitudes of the poet towards Nature. There is Wordsworth's attitude—that which recognises her as *Natura Benigna ;* there is the attitude which recognises her as *Natura Maligna*, that of the poet who by temperament exclaims with the Syrian Gnostics, ' Matter is darkness—matter is evil, and of matter is this body, and to become incarnate is to inherit sorrow and grievous pain ' ; and there is the attitude which recognises her as being neither benign nor malignant, but the cold, passionless, unloving mother to whom the sorrows, fears, and aspirations of man are indifferent because unknown—the attitude, in a word, of Matthew Arnold in his poem ' In harmony with Nature,' and other recent poets who have written after the general acceptance of the evolutionary hypothesis.

Wordsworth's influence in regard to the painting of Nature was no doubt great upon all the poets of his time, and upon none was it greater than upon Byron, who scoffed at him. In order to see Wordsworth's influence upon Byron we have only to compare the third and fourth cantos of *Childe Harold* with the first and second. But besides this, Byron was evidently in the later decade of his life a student of Wordsworth's theories as to the use of natural language instead of poetic diction. In Julia's letter in *Don Juan*, notwithstanding occasional echoes such as that of a couplet by an obscure writer, Barton Booth—

> So shakes the needle, and so stands the pole,
> As vibrates my fond heart to my fixed soul—

is an admirable illustration of Wordsworth's aphorism, ' What comes from the heart goes to the heart.' The same may be said concerning the pathetic naturalness of the Haidée episode.

Would this ever have been written as we now have it had it not been for Wordsworth's Preface ? Byron's success in passionate writing seems to have left behind it the strange notion that because there is such a thing as the fine frenzy of the poet, the more frenzy the better. But what makes Byron an important figure in the romantic revival is that, while his own draughts of romanticism were drawn from the well-springs of Scott, Wordsworth and Coleridge, it was from Byron's own reservoir that the French *Romantiques* drank. Indeed it may almost be said that to his influence was largely due that revival which, according to Banville, " made French poetry leap from the sixteenth century to the nineteenth."

Southey's voluminous and industrious work upon romantic lines is receiving at this moment less attention than it deserves. There is really a fine atmosphere of romance thrown over *Thalaba* and the *Curse of Kehama*. But the atmosphere is cold. His experiments in rhymeless metre are far from being unworthy of attention, especially as they were imitated (sometimes not very successfully) by Shelley, Matthew Arnold, W. E. Henley, and notably by the interesting poet, William Sharp (Fiona Macleod). Shelley preceded Keats by three years, but it is convenient in this survey to take Keats first in regard to this subject, as we have a great deal to say upon the influence of Shelley upon certain poets of a subsequent date.

Tennyson for the most part resisted the influence of Shelley, but was greatly influenced by the blended colour and music of Keats. The present writer has elsewhere dwelt upon the fact that, brief as was Keats's life, he who had already passed through so many halls of the poetic palace was at one time passing into yet another—the magic hall of Coleridge and the old ballads. As expressions of the highest romantic temper there are not many things in our literature to be set above *The Eve of St. Mark*, and *La Belle Dame sans Merci*.

Shelley's place in the Renascence of Wonder is peculiar. His vigorous imagination was partially strangled by his humanitarianism and ethical impulse, inherited largely from Rousseau. Of all the poets of this group he was by far the most inspired by the social upheaval of the French Revolution, and, of course, apart from his splendid work in so many kinds of poetry, he is a very important figure in the revival of romanticism broadly considered. But those poems of his dealing with subjects akin to those represented by the purely romantic work of the old ballads, *Christabel* and *The Ancient Mariner* show that in the Renascence of Wonder his place is not among the first. *Queen Mab* is not the least in touch with the spiritual world. And there is more of the pure romantic glamour in Keats's two lines—

" Charmed magic casements opening on the foam
Of perilous seas, in faery lands forlorn "—

than in the whole of *The Witch of Atlas*. It is, however, in the effect of Shelley's writings upon certain poets who succeeded him that his influence is so curious.

After Shelley's music began to captivate the world certain poets set to work upon the theory that between themselves and the other portion of the human race there is a wide gulf fixed. Their theory, in short, was that they are to sing, as far as possible, like birds of another world. Indeed, it may be said that in Philip James Bailey, Sydney Dobell and Alexander Smith, all true poets, and the first narrowly escaping becoming great, wonder ran to seed, while " acceptance " shrank to a fearfully minus quantity. It might also be said that the poetic atmosphere became that of the supreme Palace of Wonder—Bedlam.

With regard to Bailey's endowments, there are passages in his tremendous poem of ' Festus ' which fully justify all that his contemporaries, including Tennyson, prophesied for him.

As to Sydney Dobell, he, in " Balder " far outshot Bailey in extravagance, and Alexander Smith, whose ambition was—

" To shoot a poem like a comet out,
    Far splendering the sleepy realms of night "—

tried to outshoot Dobell, while Stanyan Bigg tried to outshoot them all.

But the strange thing is that these writers of Bedlamite poetry were not Bedlamites at all, but men of great common sense. This is seen in Dobell's Edinburgh lecture upon poetry, in which he said admirably, that the poet must be " the man with the perfect mind," and that " the poem is the perfect expression of that perfect mind " ; yet in " Balder," Dobell, and in the " Life Drama " Alexander Smith produced each a poem so exactly like a Bedlamite's poem, that nothing will ever now persuade the reader of this generation that they were not each more or less mad. They were on the contrary, among the sanest men of their time, and the reason why " Balder " and the " Life Drama " read like a Bedlamite's poems is this, that the writers deliberately tried to make them read so. And so poets of our own day are apt to forget in their worship of Shelley, that, admitting Dobell's theory about the poet's " perfect mind," the question still is, What kind of mind is the perfect mind ? Is it that mind which, like the mind of Homer, of Sophocles, of Shakespeare, of Goethe, is in accord with the healthy mind of general humanity ? or is it that mind which is in accord with nothing, not even with itself and the phantasms of its own conjuring ?

The country from which the followers of Shelley sing to our lower world was admirably named " Nowhere " by Bailey. And one of the most striking scenes of " Festus " would seem to show that " Nowhere " is a country of remarkable geographical peculiarities.

Browning's Sordello seems to be laid in this country of " Nowhere," and there are other splendid successes in this direction, but he soon left the region.

In such poems as " La Saisiaz " he is apt to fall into the mistake which spoilt Hamlet's life —that of trying to make the best of both these worlds.

Nineteenth century poets finding that they have two places to think about at once—the physical universe, and that which is beyond the physical universe—cannot determine which they will claim for inheritance. Having these two " wheres," " Somewhere " and " Nowhere," upon which to exercise their " perfect minds," they are vexed by an ' *embarras de richesses.*'

Both these inferences are, however, wrong. First, there is no reason whatever why a poet should be madder than the rest of us ; and, secondly, so far from " Nowhere " being his proper singing gallery, if ever there was a vocalist whose place is especially and peculiarly " Somewhere," that vocalist is the poet. " Somewhere " being the poet's home, the most awkward results naturally follow if the poet wanders, as so many poets of the romantic school do wander, into " Nowhere."

As regards, however, the French *romantiques* of the thirties to whom Banville alludes—those whose revolt against French classicism culminated, perhaps, in that great battle of *Hernani* before mentioned—their revolt was even more imperfectly equipped with knowledge of the physiognomy of mediævalism than that of Scott.

With regard to Victor Hugo, however, it may

be said that, modern as he was in temper, he was able by aid of his splendid imagination in *La Pas d'Armes du Roi Jean,* and indeed in many other poems, to feel and express the true Renascence of Wonder. But while in poetry the mere physiognomy of life is only suggested, in prose it has to be secured.

Hugo never secured it. His faculty of wonder, indeed, seems to have grown with the years, for in the second series of *La Lègende des Siècles* published in his seventy-fifth year, depicting a certain tremendous struggle "*Entre Gèants et Dieux,*" he gives us a picture of the giant Phtos, manacled and buried under Olympus by the usurping gods. Phtos breaks a hole through the bottom of the mountain, and sees certain sights which for wonder surpass all the wonderful sights seen by all our English poets put together.

> " Phtos est à la fenêtre immense du mystère.
> It voil l'autre côté monstrueux de la terre,
> L'inconnu, ce qu' aucun regard ne vit jamais,
> Des profondeurs qui sont en même temps sommets
> Un tas d'astres derrière un gouffre d'empyrées,
> Un ocean roulant aux plis de ses marées,
> Des flux et des reflux de constellation."

This in fact, is that famous " l'Infini," about which the venerable poet is calculated to have written from the publication of " *Irtamène* " downwards, fifty thousand epigrams.

" Un globe est une balle, un siècle est un moment ;
Mondes sur mondes, l'un par l'autre ils se limitent.

    *   *   *   *   *   *

O Stupeur ! il finit par distinguer, au fond
De ce gouffre, ou le jour avec la nuit se fond,
A travers l'épaisseur, d'une brune éternelle,
Dans on ne sait quelle ombre enorme, une prunelle."

Phtos then scales Olympus, and frightens the gods by crying out, " O, dieux, il est un Dieu ! "

Our object being merely to trace to its sources that stream of Romanticism upon which the poetry of the nineteenth century has been nourished, this work should properly close here. And if a word or two is said upon the poets who immediately followed the great group, it must not be supposed that any general criticism of these latter poets is attempted.

It was inevitable, no doubt, that Tennyson, a poet so absolutely voicing the Victorian age and its narrow cosmogony, who alone seemed to speak for that age, should suffer considerable decadence of fame the moment that a new epoch with a new cosmogony should begin to clamour for utterance, and undoubtedly this has been the case. Yet in virtue of the large mass of perfect work actually done he would perhaps be the greatest poet of the nineteenth century if Coleridge had not left us among his own large mass of inferior work half-a-dozen poems which will be the delight, the wonder, and the despair of English poets in all time to come. In the blending of music and colour so that each seems born of each, it is hard to think that even the poet of *The Eve of St. Agnes* and *The Ode to a Nightingale* was the superior of him who gave us *The Lady of Shalott* and *The Lotos-Eaters*. But when it comes to the true romantic glamour it cannot be said that he was instinctively in touch with the old spirit. The magnificent *Idylls of the King*, in temper as well as in style one of the most modern poems of its time, does occasionally, as in the picture of the finding of Arthur, give us the old glamour very finely. But the stately rhetorical movement of his blank verse is generally out of harmony with it. That romantic suggestion which Shakespeare's blank verse catches in such writing as we get in the fifth act of *The Merchant of Venice*, in *Pericles*, and in hundreds of other passages, shows, however, that blank verse, though not so ' right ' in romantic poetry as rhyme, can yet be made sufficiently flexible. It is only in the poetic methods of his rhymed poems that Tennyson successfully worked on romantic lines, though of course the *naïveté,* the fairy-like, unconscious grace of

Coleridge at his best, were never caught by any of his successors. And yet above all nineteenth-century poets Tennyson is steeped in the absolute humour of romanticism. In Shakespeare himself there is no finer example of absolute humour than he gives us in those lines where the " Northern Farmer " expresses his views on the immorality of Bessy Marris :

Bessy Marris's barne ! tha knaws she laäid it to meä.
Mowt a beän, mayhap, for she wur a bad un, sheä.
'Siver, I kep 'um, I kep 'um, my lass, tha mun understond,
I done moy duty boy 'um as I 'a done boy the lond.

As to Browning, in order to discuss adequately his place as regards the Renascence of Wonder a long treatise would be required. On the realistic side of the Romantic movement he is, of course, very strong. His sympathies, however, are as modern as Matthew Arnold's own, except, of course, on the theological side, where he is a century behind his great poetic contemporaries. His desire is to express not wonder but knowingness, the opposite of wonder. In a study of his works, made by the present writer many years ago, the humour of Browning was named Teutonic grotesque. The name is convenient, and nearly, though not quite, satisfactory. Perhaps Teutonic grotesque, which in architecture at least, lies in the expression of deep ideas through fantastic forms, is the only absolute grotesque. In Italian and French grotesque the incongruity throughout all art lies in a simple departure from the recognised line of beauty, spiritual or physical; but in the Teutonic mind the instinctive quest is really not —save in music—beauty at all, but the wonderful, the profound, the mysterious; and the incongruity of Teutonic grotesque lies in expressing the emotions aroused by these qualities in forms that are unexpected and bizarre. It is easy, however, to give too much heed to Browning's grotesquery in considering his relation to Romanticism. Ruskin has affirmed that such poems as *The Bishop Orders his Tomb* is the best rendering to be found in literature of the old temper, and on this point Ruskin speaks with authority.

With regard to Matthew Arnold, in *The Scholar Gypsy* he undoubtedly shows, reflected from Wordsworth, a good deal of the realistic side of Romanticism. But there is no surer sign that his temper was really " Augustan " than the fact that in his selections from Gray in Ward's *English Poets*, he actually omits the one stanza in Gray's *Elegy*, which shows him to have been a true poet—the stanza about the robin, above quoted in the remarks upon Gray. *The Forsaken Merman*, whose very name suggests the Renascence of Wonder, beautiful as it is, is quite without the glamour and magic of such second-rate poets as the author of the *Queen's Wake*, and has no kinship with Coleridge or the old ballads. As to his attitude towards Nature, it is in such poems as *Morality* and *In Harmony with Nature* that Arnold shows that he comes under the third category of nature-poets above mentioned. With regard to his humour, Arnold was essentially a man of the world—of the very modern world—and his humour, though peculiarly delicate and delightful, must certainly be called relative and not absolute.

As regards the romantic temper, two English imaginative writers only have combined a true sympathy with a true knowledge of it, and these were of more recent date—Rossetti and William Morris. They had, of course, immense advantages owing to such predecessors in literature as Meinhold, and also to the attention that had been given to the subject in Pugin's *Gothic Architecture* and in the works of other architects, English and foreign.

The poet of *Christabel* himself was scarcely

more steeped in the true magic of the romantic temper than was the writer of *The Blessed Damozel* and *Sister Helen,* while in the knowledge of romance Coleridge was far behind the later poet. With regard to humour, Rossetti and Morris hold in their poetry no place either with the absolute or relative humorists, but those who knew them intimately can affirm that personally they are both humorists of a very fine order.

The truth is, as already mentioned, that Rossetti consciously, and Morris, perhaps unconsciously, worked upon the entirely mistaken theory that in romantic poetry humour has properly no place. Those who have styled Morris unhealthy on account of his lamentations about Death are inconsistent. He was as healthy as Chaucer himself. "It is the characteristic of every conscious organism in health to want to live," says a great naturalist. Surely it is the sign of a perfectly healthy mind to lament now and then that the time is approaching faster and faster when the good things of this comfortable earth will be at an end—when there will be no more making of verses—no more pleasant translating of Sagas—no more Icelandic trips— no more companionship of friends—and even, perhaps, no more "sage greens." "The deep dishonour of death" aroused the honest indignation of Shakespeare ; and he surpasses Morris in the amount of abuse he pours upon the "spoiler of life's feast." In fact, the genuine gusto with which Morris gives vent to his wrath against Death convinces us that, besides being one of the most delightful poets that ever lived (and also one of the greatest if we properly consider what gifts went to the writing of ' Sigurd '), he is one of the healthiest, in the sense that an old Viking or an old Greek was healthy who loved life and detested, though he might not fear, death.

Into this mistake George Meredith never fell and certainly he is the last poet who can be called a " poet of acceptance." Still he does not belong in the same way to the Renascence of Wonder as Morris, Swinburne, and Rossetti do. His early book " Modern Love," is a delight to all readers, full of true passion and true everything. But it cannot be said that he fulfilled the promise of his early work. In many of his later poems, the beautiful image seems struggling and iridescent, like a fish in a net.

The difference between literature and mere word-joining is that while literature is alive, word-joining is without life, and cannot by any power be vivified. This literary life is bi-partite in prose, tri-partite in poetry ; that is to say, that while prose requires intellectual life and emotional life, poetry requires not only intellectual life and emotional life, but rhythmic life, this last being the most important of all.

Unless the rhythm of any metrical passage is so vigorous, so natural, and so free that it seems, like Swinburne's poetry, as though it could live, if need were, by its rhythm alone, that passage has no right to existence, and should, if the substance is good, be forthwith demetricized and turned into honest prose ; for, as Thoreau has pointed out, prose at its best has high qualities beyond the reach and ken of poetry, and to compensate for the sacrifice of these the metrical gains of any passage should be beyond all cavil.

In a language so powerful and yet so rude as ours—a language requiring such an infinity of manipulation before it can be worked into melodious sequences—the difficulty of producing poetry that is at once perfect in art and adequate to the motive and intellectual power of the national character is enormous.

A Greek of the time of Pericles might have nourished his genius upon all that the broadest Athenian life could afford, and yet so inherently melodious was his mother-tongue, he could have given in his verses all those subtle *nuances* of metrical effect which in more imperfect languages are the result of a lifelong study of poetry as a fine art. But, save in the cases of a few of the most illustrious names, the poets of England, and especially the poets of the nineteenth century, fail from that lack of experience of life without which poetry is but the idle tinkling of the lyre ; or else, having that experience of life, they fail because they have no time to overcome the countless technical difficulties and metrical delicacies of poetic art.

Meredith had something of an ear for iambic verse, though none for anapæstic, and yet, for some reason or another, he is fond of attempting anapæsts.

There is no more clear and sharp distinction between poets than that which divides them between poets who have the iambic ear, and poets who have the anapæstic. While writers like Keats and Wordsworth in passing from the iambic to the anapæstic movement pass at once into doggerel, writers like Shelley and Swinburne are so entirely at home in anapæstic movements that even their iambic lines seem always on the verge of leaping into the anapæstic dance.

If verse were simply quintessential prose, then assuredly Meredith would be one of the most effective poets in English literature. In the art of " packing a line " he is almost without an equal. Take the following stanzas from the poem called " Earth and Man."

> He may entreat, aspire,
>> He may despair, and she has never heed.
>> She drinking his warm sweat will soothe his need,
> Not his desire.
> She prompts him to rejoice,
>> Yet scares him on the threshold with the shroud.
>> He deems her cherishing of her best-endowed,
> A wanton's choice.

The first two lines here are much more than quintessential prose, they are poetry worthy of almost any writer in the English language. But the lines which follow are metrically bad, and bad in the worst way, for they show that the poet whose natural instinct, judging from his " *Modern Love*," is to avoid elision and to spread out the syllables of his lines after Keats's fashion, attempts an elision here without understanding what is the true nature and function of elision in English poetry. And throughout his poetry there are lines which strike upon the ear like flints :—

She fancied, armed beyond beauty, and thence grew,
In mind only, and the perils that ensue.
Hear, then, my friend, madam! Tongue-restrained he stands.

Still, notwithstanding all the rugged lines in Meredith's poetry, there are plenty of poems of his which easily show that he has a true call to express himself in metre. Perhaps " *The Lark Ascending* " is the finest of all these, though, of course, even that is without the supreme metrical inspiration of Shelley's " *Skylark* " and Swinburne's " *Sea Mew.*" And this is no faint praise, for among those who express, or endeavour to express, themselves in metre, how many have really a call to do so ?

Nothing is more inscrutable than the desire for metrical expression. Carlyle's endowment of some of the poetic qualities—such as imagination, picturesqueness, emotive eloquence—was very great ; but judging from his own doggerel verses and his ignorant and stupid talk about Keats and Shelley, his ear for music was the ear of Bully Bottom after he had been translated.

Compare, for instance, the poems of O' Shaughnessy with Meredith's poems. So rugged, harsh, and flinty are many of Meredith's lines that the reading of them would have inflicted positive physical pain on O'Shaughnessy's ear. Yet we do not hesitate to say that one or two of Meredith's poems contain more of the raw material of poetry than could have been produced by O'Shaughnessy in a lifetime. The throb of emotional and intellectual life stirs nearly every line ; whereas in O'Shaughnessy's verses we often find nothing but that rhythmic life without which no metrical writing has any *raison d'être* at all.

The truth is that in modern England poetry is not large enough for the growing limbs of life or rather our poetic forms are not large enough to cover the limbs of life and the limbs of art. Sir William Temple's comparison of life to a blanket too small for the bed was never so applicable as now. In order to pull it over one part of our bodies another part has to be left out in the cold.

Manliness and intellectual vigour combined with a remarkable picturesqueness are the most noticeable qualities of Meredith's work.

It is hard to think that even the singer of the *Ode to the West Wind* is in lyric power greater than he who wrote the choruses of *Atalanta* and the still more superb measures of *Songs before Sunrise* and *Erechtheus*. Indeed, we have only to recall the fact that before Shelley wrote it was an axiom among poets and critics that few, if any, more metres could ever be invented in order to give his proper place to a poet who has invented more metres than all the poets combined from the author of *Piers Plowman* down to the present day.

Swinburne, too, seems, consciously or unconsciously, to act upon the theory that humour is out of place in romantic poetry. For in his prose writings he shows a great deal of wit and humour. With regard to form and artistic qualities generally, a new kind of poetic diction now grew up—a diction composed mainly of that of Shelley and of Keats, of Tennyson, of Rossetti, of Swinburne, yet mixed with Elizabethan and more archaic forms—a diction, to be sure, far more poetic in its elements than that which Coleridge, Scott, and Wordsworth did so much to demolish, but none the less artificial when manipulated by a purely artistic impulse for the production of purely artistic verse. It is, we say, true enough that the gorgeous and beautiful word-spinning of writers like Arthur O' Shaughnessy, Philip Bourke Marston, and those called the Pre-Raphaelite poets is far more like genuine poetry than was the worn-out, tawdry texture of eighteenth-century platitudes in which Hayley and Samuel Jackson Pratt bedecked their puny limbs. Rossetti, the great master of this kind of poetic diction, saw this, and during the last few years of his life endeavoured to get away from it when writing his superb poems, *A King's Tragedy*, and *The White Ship*.

THE END